THE STAGING HANDBOOK

Francis Reid

A & C Black, London
Theatre Arts Books, New York

A & C BLACK (PUBLISHERS) LTD
35 Bedford Row, London WC1R 4JH

Reprinted by A & C Black 1983

First published by Pitman Publishing Ltd
1978, and published simultaneously in
the USA by Theatre Arts Books, 153 Waverly
Place, New York, NY 10014

© Francis Reid 1978

UK ISBN 0–7136–2324–1
US ISBN 0–87830–160–7

Printed and bound in Great Britain at
The Pitman Press, Bath

Contents

Acknowledgements

The author would like to express his gratitude to all those who helped by providing illustrations or allowing their work to be interrupted by the author's own camera. In particular, thanks are due to Reg Allen, Rudolf Biste, Jack Bowhill, Desmond Collins, Bill Crisp, Billy Crockett, Alistair Couborough, June Dandridge, Shirley Duff Gray, Heinz Fritz, Ian Gillespie, Freddie Grimwood, Don Hindle, Arthur Hoare, Michael Rogers, Philip Rose, Dorothy Tenham, Joe Thornley, Graham Walne, Anna Welbourne, and the unique picture archives of Rank Strand Electric and their magazine *Tabs*.

Throughout this book, the word *actor* has been used to include all performers whether male or female; and in references to technical personnel, the words *he* and *she* should be regarded as freely interchangeable. The world of theatre rejected discrimination of all kinds, including sex, long before such equality became either fashionable or a matter for legislation.

Prologue

In an ideal world, the preparation of a theatre performance would be a process of gradual evolution from script to audience. The sung or spoken word would be clothed in movement and gradually all the elements—scenery, costume, props, sound, light—would be added. The whole process would take place on the actual stage to be used for performance and would be a delicate creative process free from the scheduled rigours of budgeted money and time: a tender blossom to be revealed to its audience when, and only when, it was adjudged ready by its creators.

Reality is somewhat different from such ideals: much of the creative process takes place in rehearsal rooms far removed from the stage, time and money is always short, and was there ever a production that was considered ready by its creators?

In preparing a theatre performance, whether amateur or professional, there are normally two distinct processes—

First, the acting rehearsals (without scenery, costumes or lighting) usually carried out in a rehearsal room rather than on the stage of the theatre or hall which will house the actual performance, and

Secondly, the technical and dress rehearsals where this previously rehearsed acting performance is integrated with all the technical apparatus of the stage.

This second phase (the *staging*) is relatively complex, particularly within the context of the short time scale in which it has to be accomplished. It is therefore hardly surprising that many shows (again, both amateur and professional) which looked promising in their final run-throughs in the rehearsal room, lose something—or even fall apart—in the transfer to the stage.

This *staging* process is largely a matter of organisation and communication both prior to and during the technical and dress rehearsals. Effective staging depends upon team work. Every single member of the production team, including the actor, must have some understanding of what each department is trying to do and where its particular problems lie.

In the theatre, everyone has a streak of idealism, a yearning for perfection, and very often a single-minded pursuit of their personal speciality. Everybody, in the nicest possible way, is in it for grabs. The designer wants a lavishly executed set, the lighting man wants a huge spotlight rig, the wardrobe people have visions of lush brocades and exquisite wigs, the sound man is convinced that success can only result from a continuous multi-track birdsong and burbling brook ... and so on. Where stands the actor in all this? Or the playwright? Or, especially, the audience?

In the theatre, as in the life which it reflects, the conversion of ideals into reality inevitably involves compromise. Success usually results from careful balancing so that one element does not get out of proportion with the others. If the balance is correct, the whole can be more than just the sum of the parts: the compromise of ideals will result in an ideal compromise.

Although much of this book is written in terms of the professional theatre, its approach to the solution of staging problems is universal—these problems are common to all forms of theatre, whether they be organised on an amateur, educational or professional basis.

PART I
ORGANISING THE STAGING

1 Organisation

Efficient staging requires efficient planning and efficient planning requires some sort of organisational structure. *Organisation* is one of the more suspect words of our times. It is something that we tend to recoil from. The word has an image of corporate inefficiency: an anonymous body whose decisions, although taken in the name of logic, appear to lack simple common-sense and humanity. But organisation (the process) carried out by an organisation (the structure) is essential for the process of making a plan and implementing it. Successful organisation is closely linked to optimum size. Undersize can result in inadequate planning producing inadequate actions. Oversize can result in the generation of paper which tends to produce more paper rather than actions. Either way, there is a loss: a loss of money and a loss of time.

Organisational structure

To make and implement decisions, an organisational structure is required. There are two possibilities: a structure has to be set up, or one already exists. Neither situation is entirely satisfactory. An existing organisational structure usually has built-in defects (often people) and these defects may be virtually irremovable. On the other hand, setting up an organisation from scratch is a daunting task and even worse deficiencies may get incorporated. The imperfect organisation that you know is probably better than the (possibly) perfect organisation that you do not know. The known is something that you can learn to live with: many deficiencies, if recognised, can be turned into advantages. It is the unknown—the blank planning sheet—that holds the terror.

The traditional British or American theatre set-up is two-part: owners of theatres who rent their buildings to producers of shows. This gives rise to an *us and them* situation where any production has two sets of people and two sets of materials: *ours and theirs*. Indeed, as both parties use the words 'ours' and 'theirs' with opposite meaning, it can be quite important to realise who's who during a technical rehearsal! The situation is most obvious with a theatre company moving into a London or Touring theatre, but it also arises in a village or school hall: anyone who has dealt with a caretaker, or indeed anyone who has been a caretaker will recognise the *us and them* syndrome. Even in theatres where the bricks and mortar are owned by the show's producers, the situation can arise.

The producer's technical staff know the details of the show because they have been planning and rehearsing prior to moving on to the stage. They are the natural people to manage the operation and they must *communicate*. Most people will feel involved if they know where they are heading and by what route it is proposed to travel. Every production has to have a destination and a map. This is the only way to avoid an undercurrent, from all sides, of such muttered thoughts as 'I wish they would make up their minds', 'Here we go again', or perhaps just plain 'Obstructionists!'.

Departments

The traditional departmental divisions are into *stage* (or *scenery*), *props*, *electrics*, and *wardrobe*: and there is a substantial folklore devoted to true and apocryphal tales of finely drawn demarcation lines. Electrics is fairly easy to define once it is accepted that the handling of a chandelier is the responsibility of props when it is merely decorative, but is looked after by electrics if it actually lights up. The distinctions between scenery and props are becoming somewhat blurred with the growth of newer techniques in design and construction. Hand props and furniture are easy to classify, and the dressings on a conventional box set may also be easily recognised as props. However some of the more representational design styles produce units which are both (some cynics would say neither!). This can lead to a negative definition of props as being everything which cannot be classified as scenery, wardrobe or electrics. Even this definition places a large question mark over costume props—swords, spectacles, jewellery, and the like.

These rigid traditional divisions tend to remain only in what we may call mainstream theatre—Broadway, the West End and their supporting chains of regional touring houses. But such 'mainstream' is an ever decreasing portion of total theatre activity. 'Theatre' can cover anything and everything from a highly mechanised national repertory opera house to a performance space where the total furnishings might be only audience chairs—and sometimes not even that.

As a theatre increases in size and complexity, the departments become more specialised. For example, *flys* and *sound* become separate departments rather than specialised duties of members of the stage and electrics departments respectively. *Maintenance*, which in a small theatre is looked after by the production

staffs, becomes separate. Conversely, the smaller the theatre, the more likely are its staff to be versatile technicians able and willing to deal with everything that happens backstage.

Job titles

In trying to understand the structure of any particular organisation, the actual job titles of the personnel can be somewhat confusing. *Technical director*, for example, has been known to cover everything from the administrator at the top of a huge organisational pyramid to a jack-of-all-trades one-man-band who builds the scenery, stokes the boilers, and works the lighting switchboard with one hand while flying the house-tabs with the other. Status adjectives like *director*, *manager*, *chief*, *supervisor* and *master* are liberally bestowed in the theatre, frequently with qualifying adjectives like *general*. Apart from such terminology being in line with the larger than life ballyhoo which is an essential part of theatre, it is not unknown for an inflated job title to be offered in compensation for an inadequate salary increase.

Some of the job titles, with an indication of some of their varying job descriptions are:—

Producer
Formerly the person who directed the actors. Now more properly describes the *packager* of a show: the person who brings together script, theatre, director, possibly the star(s), but above all the money.

Director
Has the ultimate responsibility. Controls the actors directly and controls everything else indirectly through the other members of the production team (scene, costume and lighting designers, stage manager, etc). Must have ultimate veto, but should rarely be seen using it.

Designer
Responsible for the conception of all the visual elements and the supervision of their execution within an agreed budget. Where scenery, props or costumes are to be made specially, supplies a design; where anything is to be rented or borrowed, is responsible for the choice. Separate designers may be employed for scenery and costumes.

Lighting Designer
Conceives the lighting style in discussion with the director and designer, plans an appropriate equipment rig (within the budget) and supervises its installation and focusing. Composes the balance of the lighting at the lighting rehearsal and supervises its execution and modification throughout the dress rehearsals. The job is occasionally combined (particularly in America) with that of scenic designer.

Technical Director (Administrator/Manager)
Co-ordinates and budgets the work of all technical production departments. Essential in a large organisation with several productions simultaneously under way in performance and rehearsal.

Production Manager
In a big organisation (particularly one working in repertoire) responsible for the technical preparation of new productions from conception up to first performance, co-ordinating the work and budget of the organisation's own workshops and/or outside contractors and suppliers. In a smaller organisation, may also be senior stage manager and/or technician.

Stage Director
Formerly the title of the senior member of the stage management but abandoned when producers became called directors.

Stage Manager
In overall control of the performance and responsible for signalling the cues that co-ordinate the work of the actors and technicians. In the absence of the director (or an appointed deputy), the stage manager is responsible for ensuring that the production as a whole, including individual acting performances, does not make any substantial departure from the original.

Deputy Stage Manager
Often 'runs' the show from the prompt corner (giving the cues,

calling and prompting the artists) to leave the stage manager free to supervise the entire stage area and/or check out the performance from the auditorium.

Assistant Stage Managers (ASMs)
In addition to giving general assistance to the stage manager and deputy, and understudying their functions in cueing the performance, the ASMs may have responsibility for such departments as props and sound. In general the smaller the organisation, the more the ASMs have to 'do' rather than merely supervise.

Company Manager
Frequently the producer does not own the theatre where the show is being performed. The company manager is then the producer's senior representative in the theatre, liaising with the theatre management. He is usually responsible for salary payments to the company and the preparation of day-to-day accounts. Thus the company manager is the administrative line of communication between the producer and both the theatre management and the acting company. In Britain, particularly in London and touring companies, the job is often combined with the duties of stage manager.

Heads of Departments (HODs)
Usually used to denote the theatre's resident staff (particularly the master carpenter and the chief electrician) rather than the producing company's staff.

Dayman
A member of the stage staff (stage dayman) or electrics staff (electrics dayman) employed on a permanent full-time basis. Often classified as first dayman or second dayman according to seniority and experience.

Showman
A part-time member of the stage, props or electrics staff employed, usually on a casual basis, for performances only.

Master Carpenter
The senior member of the stage staff. Responsible through his management of the stage staff for the safe movement of all scenery during rehearsals and performances. Normally also responsible for the general organisation of everything in the backstage area except electrics, but including maintenance, cleanliness, safety and fire precautions.

Chief Machinist
An alternative name for master carpenter, particularly in larger theatres or opera houses with mechanised stages.

Mechanists
Alternative (particularly in Australia) for scenery handling staff.

Flyman

Supervises all flying of scenery above the stage. Normally a senior assistant of the master carpenter. Only in the biggest theatres (where the title may be *flymaster*) are the duties confined to flying.

Property Master

Senior member of the property staff. Organises the handling of props at performances. In small theatres and on small tours, this organisation of props may be in the hands of an assistant stage manager. In some production theatres, the property masters may make props in addition to dealing with performances, although in the largest theatres and opera houses there is usually a separate property-making workshop staff. The property master is often a property mistress and the title *property manager* is coming into use.

Props

Members of the property department are often referred to as just *props* rather than 'property man' or other similarly formal titles.

Chief Electrician

Senior member of the electrics department. In smaller theatres, responsible for all the electrical maintenance of the building in addition to the stage lighting. In larger theatres, deals only with the stage lighting while maintenance is handled by a house engineer. In America, called *master electrican*.

Deputy Chief Electrician
Assistant Chief Electrician

Self-explanatory. One of these is usually the operator of the lighting control 'switchboard'. In theatres with no separate sound department, another deputy or assistant would assume responsibility for sound.

Stage Electrics

Rank and file electricians who plug up equipment during scene changes, handle microphones, etc. Often part-time showmen.

Limes

Often used to describe follow-spot operators.

Sound

Is still at such a relatively young point in its growth as a separate department that job titles have not yet settled into any uniformity. The terms sound engineer, operator, consultant, supervisor are in common but not standard use.

Resident Stage Manager

In many theatres there is a traditionally uneasy truce between the master carpenter and the chief electrician: both are responsible to the theatre manager for their respective departments, but neither is in charge of the whole stage operation. In most touring theatres, the master carpenter is designated *resident stage manager* and is in overall charge of the stage, being responsible to the theatre manager for staff and building, and to the touring company manager for the performance facilities. When there is no touring stage manager (as, for example, when the theatre is playing variety), the resident stage manager assumes all stage management duties and responsibilities.

Wardrobe Mistress/Master/Manager/Supervisor
The senior person in charge of costumes. The wardrobe department has two main functions: the *making* of costumes during the production period and the *maintenance* of these costumes during the run of performances. The making may be done by outside contractors or in the theatre's own workshops. *Wardrobe manager* is a title increasingly used in the larger organisations where the senior wardrobe person has to supervise extensive costume making workshops. In this case, the title *wardrobe maintenance* is often used for the day-to-day repairing, laundry and organisation of costumes between and during performances.

Wig Master/Mistress or Perruquier
In theatres with a classical or operatic repertoire, the number of wigs requires a special department with its own departmental head.

Dressers
Members of the wardrobe performance staff (often part-time) who help individual actors with the care and changing of their costumes.

Hallkeeper
The proper title for the stage doorman. Responsible for the security of the backstage area, screening visitors, looking after keys, mail, messages, etc.

Housekeeper
Supervises the cleaning staff for the entire theatre including dressing rooms and backstage areas with the exception of the actual stage and workshops which are usually cleaned by the staff of the appropriate staging departments.

This list of job titles does not pretend to be exhaustive or absolutely accurate in what might be called the 'small print'. Many holders of these titles may even deny that their duties are as described! It is only intended to give a basic idea of broad general usage. Later chapters on individual departments give a more detailed discussion.

2 Types of organisation

Before discussing some typical organisations, we should look at theatre's great divide: 'production' and 'running'. The climax of staging is the First Performance. Events prior to this are referred to as *production* and expenses incurred are *production costs*. As the rehearsal period produces no income, the production costs are in the nature of an investment. The first performance is the start of the *running* period and the expenses are *running costs*. There is now an income from the sale of the seats and this has to cover not just the running costs but a proportion of the production costs equivalent to at least the total of these production costs divided by the number of performance weeks. Additionally if the capital finance for the production costs has been raised by commercial means, the income will be required to produce a profit at a rate reflecting the high risk nature of the investment. Box office income, even from a full house, is frequently inadequate to cover the costs of a theatre performance—particularly the production costs and often the running costs also. The question of augmenting income with a subsidy is discussed in the next chapter.

But the matter of costs and their budgeting is only one aspect of the divide between the production and running periods: the personnel required will vary not just in numbers but in degree of specialisation—and in personality. There can be a tendency among technical staff to find the production period much more exciting than performance and this is understandable, particularly in the case of a play with a permanent set and few sound or light cues. But the performance is (and must be) the climax—not just the first performance but every performance. The 'system' often favours production staffs in terms of status and salary, but the theatre has at least equal need of the technician whose speciality is to play his part in the meticulous running of the ninety-ninth performance.

Producers without theatres

Production organisations can be surprisingly small, lacking both staff and hardware assets. London producers, eminently successful in both financial and artistic terms, have been known to operate from a pair of small offices housing the producer himself, a production manager, a business manager and a secretary.

The function of such a producer is to bring together the best possible team to realise a particular script. He starts with a mutually compatible director and star(s), then, with their approval, goes on to select key production personnel from the large available freelance pool. Where possible, this production team is constructed from those whose sympathies and experience seem appropriate and who seem likely to be able to work well together, often because they have done so successfully in the past. With a theatre of appropriate size, type and location in mind, the whole package is budgeted to present an investment attraction in the traditional theatrical mould of potential high profit at certain high risk. As rising costs force theatrical financing away from private investment towards public subsidy, the financing becomes a matter of budgeting for a certain but calculated and restricted loss. Either way, each show that such a producer puts together is virtually an independent company and its accountancy is much simplified if each show negotiates with outside contractors to buy production hardware such as scenery and costumes, and to rent running hardware such as lighting equipment, sound equipment and perhaps props.

Non-producing theatres

Non-producing theatres require the smallest staffs. All construction is done in outside contractors' workshops and brought to the theatre as a ready-to-assemble package. Extra casual staff can be hired to augment the theatre's small stage crew, and for the first fit-up at least one of the workshop carpenters will be present. For subsequent moves to other theatres, the fit-up would be supervised by a touring carpenter. Contemporary decor styles for plays usually require few, if any, scenic changes during the performance: where changes are necessary, they tend to be confined to flying or other re-arrangements of scenic elements within a permanent framework.

In such a theatre the resident staff might be around six: a master carpenter and a chief electrician, each with two assistants. The carpenter's assistants would double as property master and flyman respectively, although in such a set-up there is a considerable degree of overlap between duties as days off tend to reduce the number of staff in the theatre to five or four. When necessary, the staff is augmented for performances by showmen who are normally part-timers, following another occupation by day.

Musicals require a larger staff but in a non-producing theatre this is mainly a performance requirement met by a large show staff. There is normally also a slightly larger permanent day-staff, perhaps up to eight or ten, because musicals are performed in larger theatres where more staff are required for maintenance.

The non-producing theatres present 'runs' of shows: either the short fixed one- or two-week runs of the touring system, or the open-ended runs of West-End or Broadway where it is hoped that every show will run as long as 'The Mousetrap'. Runs have labour-intensive peaks—get-ins, performances, and get-outs—with relative quiet in between. The system of part-time casual showmen is the only economic way to deal with these peaks of activity, and indeed some of the most dedicated and skilled technicians are to be found amongst the part-timers of the regional touring theatres.

Producing theatres

The work pattern of a producing theatre is rather different. The labour requirement is more evenly distributed with fewer peaks of labour-intensive activity. There are three basic ways in which the performances can be organised: *repertory*, *repertoire*, *stagione*.

In *repertory*, the production has a run of limited length and planning usually requires that the length of this run be decided before the opening night. At any given time there is normally one production in performance, another in rehearsal, and several in varying degrees of planning. At the conclusion of the run of performances, the scenic hardware is normally dispersed with re-usable items being returned to stock.

In *repertoire*, several productions are available for performance during any particular period. Several performances of the same production may be given on adjacent days or there may be a changeover every single day with perhaps a gap of up to a couple of weeks between two performances of a particular work. This situation often arises in opera houses, particularly where as in Germany, many of the seats are sold on seasonal subscriptions which guarantee that by attending for example on every alternate Tuesday, a subscriber will see the entire season's repertoire of opera, ballet and drama. Thus, in any given short period, several productions may be in performance and several more in active rehearsal. At the end of a season of performances, complete sets, props, costumes, etc., are usually stored for future revival.

Stagione is rather like repertoire except that, at any given time, there is a very small range of productions in performance. A production is given intensive rehearsal, followed by a burst of performances close together, then placed in store. Each time that it is revived, it is rehearsed—often with major cast changes—almost as if it were a new production. Under the stagione system, there are fewer productions in performance and rehearsal with resultant simplification in most organisational matters, particularly casting and technical stage changeovers. It is hardly surprising that a higher standard of performance becomes possible. In opera houses, where a performance

Spielplanvorschau für Dezember 1974

GROSSES HAUS KLEINES HAUS

	Grosses Haus	Abo	Zeit	Tag/Datum	Zeit	Abo	Kleines Haus
*	Premiere: Boccaccio, Operette von Franz von Suppé	● frei	20.00	So 1.12.			
*	Wie es euch gefällt, Komödie von William Shakespeare	Ju-Ri B	19.30	Mo 2.12.	19.30	Ju-Ri A	Der Tod des Handlungsreisenden, von Arthur Miller
*	Wie es euch gefällt	CTG A + frei	20.00	Di 3.12.			
*	Boccaccio	CTG B + frei	20.00	Mi 4.12.	20.00	Mi-Abo + frei	Der Talisman, von Johann Nepomuk Nestroy
*	Gastspiel: Majestäten, von Jean Anouilh	● Do + frei	20.00	Do 5.12.			
*	Gastspiel: Majestäten	● Fr A + frei	20.00	Fr 6.12.	19.30	Ju-Ri E	Der Tod des Handlungsreisenden
*	Gastspiel: Majestäten	● frei	20.00	Sa 7.12.	20.00	Sa-Abo + frei	Der Talisman
*	Nathan der Weise, von Gotthold Ephraim Lessing	Sch s + frei	20.00	So 8.12.	20.00	frei	Der Talisman
*	Wie es euch gefällt	Ju-Ri E	19.30	Mo 9.12.			
	Im weißen Rößl, Operette von Benatzky	Di + VoBü + frei	20.00	Di 10.12.			
*	3. Symphoniekonzert – Gastkonzert des Philharmonischen Orchesters Enschede (Werke von Mozart, Strawinsky. Debussy)	Mi-Abo + frei	20.00	Mi 11.12.			
*	3. Symphoniekonzert – Gastkonzert des Philharmonischen Orchesters Enschede (Werke von Mozart, Strawinsky. Debussy)	Do-Abo + frei	20.00	Do 12.12.	19.30	Ju-Ri A	Die tollen Zwanziger, Eine literarisch-musikalische Revue
	Gastspiel: Majestäten	● frei	20.00	Fr 13.12.	20.00	frei	Popkonzert
*	Wie es euch gefällt	Sa A + frei	20.00	Sa 14.12.	20.00	frei	Ballettabend (Werke von Prokofjew, Mahler, Bartók)
*	Im weißen Rößl	CTG F + frei	20.00	So 15.12.			
*	Im weißen Rößl	VoBü + frei	20.00	Mo 16.12.	20.00	Pr-Abo + frei ●	Premiere: Elektra, Tragödie von Sophokles
				Di 17.12.	19.30	Ju-Ri A	Die tollen Zwanziger
	Nathan der Weise	Sch w + frei	20.00	Mi 18.12.	20.00	frei	Ballettabend
	Im weißen Rößl	CTG C + frei	20.00	Do 19.12.			
				Fr 20.12.	19.30	Ju-Ri B	Zum 25. Mal: Der Tod des Handlungsreisenden
	Boccaccio	Sa B + frei	20.00	Sa 21.12.	20.00	frei ●	Premiere: Die Stühle, von Eugène Ionesco
	Boccaccio	SoNa + VoBü + frei	15.30	So 22.12.	20.00	frei	Elektra
				Mo 23.12.	20.00	frei	Die Stühle
				Di 24.12.			
	Premiere: Der Rosenkavalier, Oper von Richard Strauss	● Mi + VoBü + frei	19.00	Mi 25.12.	20.00	frei	Der Talisman
*	Im weißen Rößl	frei	20.00	Do 26.12.	20.00	frei	Die tollen Zwanziger
*	Don Giovanni, Oper von Wolfgang Amadeus Mozart	Fr C + frei	19.30	Fr 27.12.	20.00	frei	Die Stühle
*	Brüderchen und Schwesterchen *)		11.00, 14.00, 17.00	Sa 28.12.			
*	Der Rosenkavalier	CTG F + frei	19.00	So 29.12.	20.00	frei	Elektra
*	Wie es euch gefällt	CTG D + frei	20.00	Mo 30.12.	20.00	frei	Mensk sien mott de Mensk, Plattdeutsche Komödie von Günther Siegmund
	Im weißen Rößl	frei	15.00	Di 31.12.	15.00	frei	Die tollen Zwanziger
	Im weißen Rößl	frei	19.00		19.00	frei	Die tollen Zwanziger

*) Alle weiteren Termine des Musicals für Kinder siehe umseitig   ÄNDERUNGEN VORBEHALTEN

Die Vorstellungen im Kleinen Haus beginnen ab 1. Dezember (von Ausnahmen und Jugendvorstellungen abgesehen) generell um 20.00 Uhr.

* Termine des Kindermusicals „Brüderchen und Schwesterchen" siehe Rückseite

Typical month's programme of a small German city's repertoire theatre with its own resident company presenting opera, plays, musicals, dance and concerts.

involves certain financial loss even in a capacity house, an extreme form of stagione is sometimes operated where only one opera is performed at a time and the theatre remains closed on evenings between these performances. This eliminates much of the costs and technical complications of daily changeovers.

In general (although the theatre world thrives on exceptions), producing theatres attempt to have all construction work carried out in their own workshops rather than by contractors. In repertory, where the productions are mounted for short runs and there are no daily changeovers, the stage and props staff can be available for some daytime construction work. The pressures of repertoire, on the other hand, normally require a completely different workshop staff to be employed. Either way, producing theatres require much bigger staffs and an altogether more complex organisation to bring the various staging elements together in the right place and time—and at the right cost.

3 Budgeting and scheduling

The key words in the organisation of successful staging are *budgeting* and *scheduling*: the management of money and the management of time. To strive towards minimum expenditure of both is a right and proper objective, but it is not enough. Once again, minimum is not necessarily optimum: success is getting the correct *balance* between the many different ingredients in the staging mix.

Budgeting and scheduling are therefore the *proportioning* of money and time. The documents produced by this process—the budgets and the schedules—have two functions. They are the means of working towards staging decisions, and they are the means of communicating these decisions.

Budgeting

Theatre financing has always been precarious: although many fortunes have been made, many many more have been lost. To the economist, a theatre performance is a labour-intensive, short-life product with an unpredictable sales volume from a grossly under-used prime retail site.

The larger forms of theatre, particularly opera, have always required a deficit-budgeting approach: without even considering the material costs, the number of people involved is such that the box-office income from a full-house cannot cover the salaries involved. It is, of course, possible to raise seat prices towards economically realistic levels, but, as seat prices rise, there is a proportionate fall in the number sold. In any case, contemporary society has accepted that there should be some attempt to make the performing arts available to all income groups.

Apart from the hit Broadway or West-End musical (and there are many more flops than hits), it is now virtually impossible to

produce any form of theatre without subsidy. The last apparently unsubsidised theatre is the comedy or whodunit with a cast no larger than half-a-dozen and no change of scene. But even this usually has some hidden form of subsidy: a 'try-out' in a subsidised regional theatre may have reduced the risk of failure and may even have met some of the production costs; the theatre building is available for rent at less than its true market figure because planning regulations prevent its redevelopment; and many actors and technicians provide a hidden subsidy by working, through love of the theatre, for less financial reward than would be regarded as adequate in other walks of life.

Thus most theatre operations have two sources of income: *earned* and *unearned*, corresponding to *box-office* and *subsidy*. The danger is that there seems to be a great psychological divide. As soon as a theatre starts to receive subsidised income, there can be a temptation for financial control to become a little less stringent, a little less urgent; for ideals to be pursued with an ever decreasing consideration for cost. Throughout life, ideals have to be tempered with reality and the theatre is no different.

Indeed, restrictions often provide the very stimulus for successful creative activity—often, but not always. We are back to our basic quest for that *optimum* which, in financial terms as in everything else, is rarely the maximum or the minimum. There is a hoary old managerial joke reply to the request for production expenses; 'Shall I see it from the box office?' This is still valid if we transform the old literal meaning of 'Will it bring people into the theatre?' to 'Will it help the audience to understand and enjoy the play?'

A staging budget has two components: production costs and running costs. As previously discussed, the production costs include all the expenditure incurred up to the first night, while the running costs are the performance expenses. Production

Many of the producing theatres now play in new exciting forms of theatre such as the Royal Exchange Theatre in Manchester.

costs and running costs interact. Sometimes an increase in production cost will cause an increase in running cost, sometimes a decrease. For example, more elaborate scenery may require more staff to handle it during performance. On the other hand, production expenditure on a certain amount of mechanisation may reduce the number of performance staff.

It is not enough for a budget to be realistic: it must be *agreed* to be realistic by all those who have to operate within it. It should not be the secret document that it nearly always is. Unfortunately it is very common for each department to be told only their own maximum figure: there is no communication of the total sum allowed for a production, nor of the inter-departmental breakdown. In an activity so dependent on team-work, there just has to be more corporate decision making—although there will normally be a point where the person carrying the financial responsibility (often the production manager with the backing of the theatre director) will have to decree 'Enough, enough, this is what we are going to agree!' Each department can then go off, knowing how they fit in to the general scheme and being in a position to say 'I told you so' at a later date. Budgets have to be progressed and reviewed at frequent intervals during the production period: requirements change and develop during rehearsal. It is therefore wise to include a substantial *contingency* amount in the total figure.

The budgeting of staging costs varies between types of theatre. A producer without his own theatre will have to cost every single item of the production. However, as he will almost certainly deal with a small number of contractors, the budgeting will be in largish block sums. For example, having established a total contract price for the scenery construction, the detailed costing of labour and materials becomes the contractor's worry. Similarly the lighting contractor's price will include the difficult-to-predict cost of blown-lamp replacement. Naturally, the contractor's figures are high to allow a margin for miscalculation, but the producer knows exactly where he stands and budgeting is reduced to block figures, with fewer imponderables and less need for large contingency allowances. The contractors have, in fact, taken over some of the risk.

In a producing theatre with its own workshop facilities, budgeting often becomes detailed cost control of materials. The labour content is usually salaried and a fixed cost—its economical use therefore becomes a matter for scheduling rather than budgeting. If the work cannot be done by scheduling existing labour, then a decision must be taken in terms of the available options: overtime, temporary additional staff, part use of contractors, simplified staging.

Every theatre organisation is different and whether these differences are fundamental or more subtle, every organisation needs its own detailed individual budgeting approach—but there are certain common hazards to be borne in mind:

* There are only certain areas where cost control can be exercised: for example, in a Mozart opera you cannot cut the second

bassoon but there is a possibility of economising on the wigs (although there are people, including not only wig-specialists, but also directors, who would cheerfully eliminate half the orchestra rather than have one chorus hair less than perfect!).

* As the opening performance approaches, there is an atmosphere of mounting hysteria where money becomes irrelevant in the minds of those whose life has become temporarily but totally obsessed by the horizons of the production. Production managers cannot remain completely cool and detached through this phase (if they do, they are likely to have a less than ideal temperament for dealing with theatre people) but they must remain cool enough to restrict last-minute financial hysteria to a sensible spending of any remains of the contingency allowance in the original budget.

* There is a psychological barrier at the point where a theatre becomes dependent on subsidy rather than box-office income alone. As soon as this barrier is broken through, there is a tendency for budget thinking to move from 'How much can we afford to spend?' to 'How much do we need to spend?' Artistically this may be a much more desirable situation: but how do we define 'need'?

* In general, theatre people are not very good at figures. Their estimates are produced in a spirit of optimism. It is surely better to go for a pessimistic estimate: there is no greater pleasure than achieving an artistic success, and doing it under budget.

Scheduling

In theatre, there is no such thing as late delivery of the finished product. The customers (audience) have contracts (tickets) and, at the appointed hour on the appointed day, they come to collect the product (performance) in person. Therefore, the first scheduling decision must be to determine the date of the opening performance. There are strong economic pressures to have this as early as possible. A theatre without performances (known as a *dark* theatre) is a very expensive place; but a theatre to which no one comes because the performances are bad is even more expensive. Artistic pressures to delay the opening as long as possible exist to counter these economic pressures to open as soon as possible. This indicates the compromise: open as soon as is feasible without prejudicing the quality of the production. A decision that requires rather fine judgement a long time in advance—perhaps before rehearsals have even commenced.

Another key date is the beginning of the technical fit-up on stage. This date varies according to the type of theatre. In a repertoire theatre, the technical and dress rehearsals must be slotted into the performance schedule of current productions. In this case, the staging period will probably extend over at least a couple of weeks and the early technical rehearsals may be carried out with some of the settings, props, wardrobe, and lighting unfinished.

The more common case—especially in British and American theatre, both professional and amateur—is the 'run' where only one production is in performance at any given time. From the moment of the *get-in* to the theatre, the stage is totally committed to the preparation of the production for its run. The fundamental staging period to be scheduled is therefore the time available between the get-in and opening performance. Naturally, for this staging period to work efficiently, the time leading up to it has to be carefully scheduled so that every possible preparation is completed in readiness for the moment of getting in.

Scheduling, therefore, involves two countdowns: first, to the get-in and, secondly, to the performance. The countdown to the get-in is possibly the simpler: to a large extent, individual departments are working on their own. The need is to ensure that each department reaches a state of maximum preparedness by the big day. The countdown between get-in and first performance depends on *integration*. Apart from completing any individual departmental work that can only be completed on the stage, the principal need is the co-ordination of departments. Certain things must be done in the correct sequence, or rather, overlapping sequence.

The scientific approach to scheduling would be by critical path analysis, with its attendant bar charts, pert charts and supporting jargon. However, a sensitivity for theatre and an aptitude for critical paths are rarely found within the same person. Satisfactory scheduling can be accomplished by more empirical methods where decisions are made on the basis of experience plus just a touch of that creative guesswork which has to be the basis of so many decisions in areas as subjective as the performing arts.

Some of the problems of scheduling will be discussed later, in the context of the problems of the different stage departments and different types of production. Meanwhile, a few of the commoner hazards may be listed:

* Schedules are not imposed: they are agreed. A successful schedule must not only be realistic, it must be *agreed* by all participants to be realistic—even if agreement has been reached, as it will be, with some reluctance.

* It is rarely possible (no, let's face it—never possible) to allocate enough time to meet the ideal requirements of each of the staging departments. In place of the ideal of 'What do we want to achieve?', the approach often has to become 'What have we time to achieve?'.

* Whereas it may be a justifiable risk to hope that five hours' work can be squeezed into four by special effort, it is improvident to plan to compress eight into four.

* Individual theatre people vary in their ability to estimate time: their estimates are often excessively optimistic or excessively pessimistic.

* Forget such conventional showbiz rhubarb as 'it'll be all right on the night' or 'a bad dress rehearsal means a good first night.'

PART II
THE STAGING DEPARTMENTS

4 Stage management

The stage management co-ordinate the work of all the staging departments; and if any of these departments does not exist in a particular production set-up, then the stage management must also carry out the duties of that missing department. Thus, in an ideal world, the stage management would only have to manage; but, in reality, they usually have to 'do' as well.

The functions and duties of the stage management fall into four main periods: *rehearsal room*, *fit-up*, *dress rehearsal*, and *performance*.

Rehearsal room

Rehearsal room activities are not strictly the concern of this book, but the stage management's organisational functions at this point may be summarised as:

(a) Scheduling rehearsals
The SM assists the director to devise a logical working schedule which makes the best use of the actor's time in accordance with contracts, union agreements, and humanity. In accordance with this schedule, the SM is then responsible for:

(i) Calling artists (i.e. notifying them of time, place, and probable duration of each rehearsal).

(ii) Booking suitable rehearsal rooms.

(iii) Calling rehearsal pianists for musical shows.

(iv) Arranging costume fittings and informing artists, costumiers and designer of these arrangements.

(v) Liaising with specialist departments such as lighting and sound as to suitable times when they can see run-throughs.

(b) Running rehearsals

    (i) Marking out the rehearsal room floor to indicate the geography of the scenery, and obtaining such substitute furniture and properties as may be necessary for rehearsal purposes.

    (ii) Recording the 'moves' in the prompt copy and constantly updating to include the continuous changes that are an inevitable part of the rehearsal process.

    (iii) Prompting with delicacy but with increasingly detailed firmness as rehearsals develop.

    (iv) Noting significant features of the developing production and informing other staging departments —particularly props.

    (v) Keeping the director in touch with the hard realistic facts of the agreed sets, costumes and props that are now being built and for which there is neither time nor money to transform into the scenic fantasies that are blossoming with the development of the actors' characterisations.

    (vi) Divining the moment when the director and cast will require support from the tea and coffee pots—and producing such refreshment dead on cue.

    (vii) Providing shoulder(s) for director and cast to cry on.

Getting in and fitting up

If the production is fully equipped with a complete set of competent departmental heads for scenery, lighting, sound, props, etc., the stage management team will need only to co-ordinate these departmental heads who will supervise the work of their staffs. The success of the co-ordination rests primarily on pre-planning: on the achievement, prior to getting into the theatre, of an agreed realistic schedule. However good the schedule, the deadening hand of *unforeseen circumstances* will be omnipresent and the SM will have to chair many an impromptu inter-departmental meeting to revise a slipping schedule.

In particularly large organisational setups with production manager and/or technical director, the stage management will have to keep only a watching brief during the fit-up—keeping a particular eye on the interests of the director and actors who tend to be forgotten at this intensive and critical point in the technical proceedings.

In the smallest organisations, the stage management, of course, not only organises but 'does': and to organise the total job while actually doing part of it is much more difficult than standing aside and taking a calculated view of the total progress.

In a medium-sized operation, the areas which particularly require SM-assisted decision-making include 'deading the borders': deciding on a compromise height for the masking borders to satisfy the often conflicting ideals of the designer, master carpenter, and lighting designer. The department which most frequently needs assistance from the stage management in the early days is props—particularly the unpacking and setting out of the hand props which have been in use during the final days in the rehearsal room.

Demarcation

A stage manager in an amateur or small professional theatre does not have to worry about demarcation between the main departments of scenery, props and electrics. Fortunately in most larger theatres, the divisions are friendly and elastic although there is a certain amount of good-natured banter between departments. Critical areas include the orchestra pit—there are some theatres where the stage staff provide the rostra for the conductor and drummer, the prop men supply chairs and the electricians plug-up the music stands. The quick-change room is another area open for integration: the carpenter provides a couple of old flats, the propman a table, mirror and chair, and the electrician a light. All this—and moving pianos—is an area where the SM needs to exercise his characteristic organisational tact.

The stage management team

Perhaps now is the moment to discuss the membership of the stage management team. A very small-scale show can be stage managed by two people—but never less than two because it is essential for the senior stage manager to be covered by an understudy. Most shows have a team of at least three: the *stage manager (SM)* in charge and as far as possible free from specific performance tasks: a *deputy stage manager (DSM)* who actually runs the show and gives the cues to all departments; and at least one *assistant stage manager (ASM)*. The number of ASMs depends on the size and type of show; often there will be just one whose main occupation, at least in rehearsals and early performances, will be to supervise props. On big shows, it is often advisable to have an ASM in charge of each side of the stage, and on tour it is usual to include the working of taped sound effects in ASM duties. Touring generally requires a largish and competent stage management team, as they have to take a different theatre staff through the show every Monday night without rehearsal.

In some respects, the stage management are like commissioned officers in the armed services: an ASM passes instructions to a master carpenter in the way that a subaltern commands a Regimental Sergeant Major. Although the ASM would appear above the master carpenter in an organisational tree chart, it is a position that has to be secured and maintained by the exercise of what can only be called personality.

Company management

The senior stage manager often combines the duties of company manager and carries the responsibility for the day to day financial affairs of the production, including payment of salaries. The actual duties of the company manager vary with the type of production company who are presenting the show, but essentially a company manager is the link man between head office and the cast and staff of the production.

Acting stage managers

There was a tradition for many years that the junior members of the stage management team were people with acting rather than technical ambitions. Apart from some situations where the ASMs are engaged for their understudying abilities, the practice appears to be dying out. This is probably a good thing for the profession of stage management, but perhaps not so good for young actors for whom a period of stage management at the beginning of their careers provided a useful priming in wider theatre problems. Certainly, any young ASM would be well advised to grab at any chance of 'walking-on' in the occasional small part: this is very useful in gaining an understanding of the actor's problems.

Allocating dressing rooms

A sensitive area and a duty that can normally be performed satisfactorily only if the stage manager knows the actors' 'pecking order' as represented by the salaries—or has become expert in divining the precise nuances of actor billing. But at least the professional has some facts to go by: there have been amateur theatre companies where less tangible features such as local prestige and committee seniority have been known to be involved. The real problems arise when a minor character has many complex costume changes and there is only one decent room close to the stage. If it is a case of the male star making way for a lady, then an appeal to gallantry usually produces results. The other way round is not so easy: perhaps a tactful reminder of women's lib is required! Either way, blessed is the stage manager who has only two communal dressing rooms in his theatre.

Lighting rehearsals

Organisation of lighting rehearsals is discussed in later chapters, but it must be emphasised that this is a moment during the pre-dress rehearsal preparation when the stage manager and his deputy must be present, giving their full undivided attention to the proceedings. It is only by full involvement in this phase of the lighting that they will understand the reasoning behind the cues and be able to cope with problems, particularly of re-setting knocked lanterns, in the later absence of the director and lighting designer.

Technical dress rehearsal

The first dress rehearsal has various names—it can be called a technical-dress, a stagger-through, a stopping-dress, etc. Whatever it is called, the intention is to sort out technical problems as they affect both actor and technician (and musicians if any). This involves a lot of stopping. Apart from major matters like scene changes and complex light cues, it will be the first time that actors have had to deal with such things as doors and windows. The Stage Manager must be in absolute command of the stage end of rehearsal. Although it will often be the director who shouts 'stop!', it must always be the SM who says 'start'. And he must do so only after every department has been informed of which cue-state the rehearsal is restarting from, and has reported back that they are ready. In particular, electrics and sound require time to 'go back'. If a scene change goes wrong, it must be the SM who decides whether it is necessary to do it again or whether a 'talk-out' has solved the problem.

And it is the SM who must ensure that the director and actors do not let the technical rehearsal slip into a 'change-the-production' session. If there are complex production moves to be revised, then it is a matter for notes and perhaps back to the rehearsal room tomorrow while the technicians use the stage to clean up *their* problems.

If the show is very simple, the length of the technical rehearsal may be reduced by 'topping and tailing'. That is, chunks of dialogue and action can be cut out when such sections of the show do not involve cues. However, this is only worthwhile if such sections are quite lengthy. Otherwise the process of stopping and restarting often takes longer than letting the rehearsal run on. By the end of the technical dress, everyone should know what is *supposed* to happen and have it plotted.

Dress rehearsals

It is only in a continuous non-stopping dress rehearsal that it can finally be discovered whether what is supposed to happen is actually possible. In some departments, such as electrics, props and effects, it is the time between cues that is the limiting factor. At a dress rehearsal, stops should only be made if disaster occurs—and the restart must be made from a point well before the point of disaster. At dress rehearsals, the stage management will perform their duties as in performance: the SM is in complete charge. The director's function is to keep silent and take notes.

Giving cues

The traditional method of giving cues has been by cue light: a red signal for stand-by and a green for go. In busy musical shows, buzzers have often been used as an alternative to greens for flys and electrics, as it is difficult for these departments to stand-by physically while concentrating on a cue light. In fact it is easier for all departments to work on verbal cues and for any size of professional show it has now become standard practice for the DSM to give cues to all departments by voice over an open sound system. The system is open in the sense that all

departments hear each other's cues: this leads to a fuller under-standing of the whole show and the picking-up of a rhythm between, for example, flys and electrics in a dissolve through a gauze.

It is important that in giving these cues, the DSM says the operative word GO as the last word in the instructional sen-tence—i.e. 'flys cue 25 (pause) GO'. With 'go flys cue 25 please', it is difficult to know the precise moment of action and there is a loss of that second stand-by on which the flyman would normally tension his muscles.

The usefulness of the hand cue should not be overlooked when a stage manager is close to the technician being cued —this is often the case with house tabs for example. The convention is to raise the hand for stand by and drop with a fast sweeping motion for the go.

A traditional prompt corner: the Old Vic, 1950. The prompt corner is basically a communications centre. In many of the newer theatres, a desk such as that on the left is mounted on castors so that it can be moved to the most appropriate position for the stage manager to see the stage action of any particular production.

Prompt book

The stage management bible is the prompt book. It has two functions: first to form a complete record of the production and secondly to provide a running reference point for giving the cues in performance. Since the cues have to be read in what might be described as 'real time', prominence is given to them—often by the use of coloured pencils. The actual 'book' itself can be made in various ways: perhaps most often by interleaving with blank pages in a ring binder. The basic requirement is to have a blank page facing every text page.

In very complex musical shows, there may be so many cues that it is difficult to cope with a traditional prompt copy during performance and it is simpler to use a sequence cue sheet. Whichever method is used, it is essential that the prompt copy be easy to read by all members of the SM team and kept safely in the theatre overnight (but not left in the prompt corner).

Performance

In performance, the DSM stays in the corner, the ASM(s) roam the stage checking and double checking, and the stage manager pops between stage and auditorium. All members of the team are continually anticipating disaster, have thought about all the possible but improbable things that could go wrong, and have planned how they will extricate the show from such disasters. The senior stage manager will usually be on stage at critical moments like curtain up and curtain calls, but will spend part of each performance watching from the auditorium to ensure that the actors remain faithful to the original production.

Stage management is, in essentials, about controlling people rather than things. A good stage manager has to be so technically competent that he can solve staging problems almost subconsciously. This allows him to give full concentration to the management of people—both acting people and technical people.

There are many ways of marking up a prompt copy including the use of separate coloured pencils for each department's cues. This example is just one method of marking but it indicates the range of information that has to be recorded.

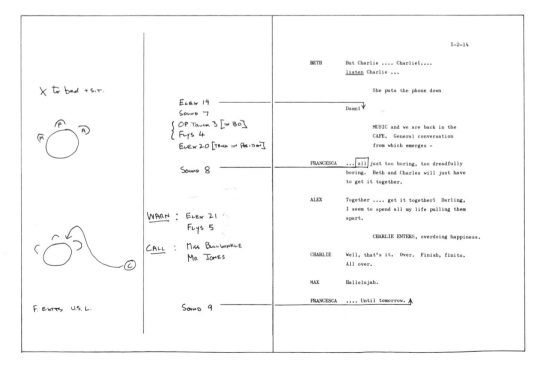

5 Scenery

Our concern in this book is with practicalities rather than aesthetics—with the practical realisation of a scenic design rather than the ideas which have determined that design's form and style.

This does not mean that the scene-designers, scene-builders, and scene-shifters should work in non-communicating cells. A scenic designer will not get very far if he does not understand something of the way in which scenery is built and moved. And those who build and move scenery will communicate more easily with the designer if they have an interest in, and knowledge of, the design process.

The available stage and its facilities, the available money and time are certainly factors that must be considered in establishing the form of scenery. This is not necessarily a heavy restriction on the designer's creativity. Within the limitations of the quantities, shapes and movements of scenic elements it is still possible to design in a wide range of styles.

Hidden scenic costs

When accusations of scenic extravagance are made, theatres often respond by pointing out that the major part of their budget is devoted to salary costs and that the outlay on scenic materials is a very small portion of total expenditure. However, a small increase in the complexity of scenery can produce a larger increase in running costs due to the extra labour and/or time required to set up the scenery before the performance and move it during the performance. This is particularly true of theatres performing in repertoire with daily changeovers: a significant proportion of total personnel costs can be attributed to the complexities of the daily changeover—often requiring overtime and overnight working.

Indeed there may be a case for incurring extra production costs to build the scenery in a way that will make its handling less labour intensive in performance. *All* the financial implications must be considered seriously in the early stages of a scenic design.

Cost-effectiveness

To help control costs, it is useful to have as detailed a breakdown as possible of the individual scenic costs, particularly if the design has to be trimmed to come within budget. It is surprising just how often the more expensive items of detailing on a set can be the least effective in communicating the production's intentions to the audience. Comparisons of cost and effectiveness can be a useful approach to keeping scenic design within budget.

Masking

In most productions the technical areas of the stage are hidden from audience view. This *masking* often has to be added—almost as an afterthought—by the technical staff using neutral borders at the top and legs or wings at the side. Masking, however, should be part of the design and good masking not only conceals the technical areas but defines the performance area. Ideally a scene design will be self-masking. The various elements of the setting will define what the audience should see and conceal what they should not—perhaps with just the addition of a high border and a couple of discreet black legs for the benefit of those in the really difficult masking positions, the end seats of the front rows. A currently popular design format is a permanent masking surround which gives unity to a series of scenes defined by the minimum of representational objects. Either way, masking is not something to be left to chance but should be worked out in plan and section on the drawing board by checking lines of sight from extreme seating positions. Some production styles deliberately leave some technical areas (often lighting equipment) unmasked—but the amount of unmasked area should be a calculated decision rather than left to chance.

Standing or changeable

If the action of a script does not require changes in location, the performance will require only one set. If this set is for a run of performances on one stage, it may be constructed from relatively heavy materials and fixed together by relatively unsophisticated means. If it is to be toured, however, or played in repertoire, light construction and speedy assembly are advisable in the interests of budgeting and scheduling. In the case of scenery changed during a performance, sophisticated construction becomes essential rather than merely advisable and the time and staff available for the scene-change will determine the degree of sophistication required.

There has been a move away from completely changeable

scenery where 'scene-change' means a complete replacement of everything behind the proscenium. This is not due entirely to economics (although cost considerations do play a large part in restricting the amount of scenery) but results largely from the aesthetic aim of establishing style by the presence from scene to scene of constant unifying elements. Consequently much of today's scenery tends to consist of a basic standing set with changeable elements.

Scenery movements

Scenery changes can be hidden from the audience (by a curtain or by a blackout) or they can be incorporated as part of the production. Scenery moving in view (an old technique enjoying a revival) should be designed and built to move without visible human assistance. Costumed staff or actors can assist a visual change but such a change is usually more effective if the assistance appears to be delicate rather than heavy load bearing.

Vertical or horizontal

Scenery can be moved vertically or horizontally. On the huge Central European stages, complete scenes can be lowered into the basement and some smaller simpler stages around the world have various elevators and traps which allow a limited lowering of parts of the scene. In most cases, however, vertical movement of scenery means hoisting upwards into a fly tower above the stage.

Horizontal movement of scenery to storage spaces (scene docks) at the side of the stage can be done manually by planning the set so that it can be broken down into pieces which can be carried, preferably by not more than two men. Alternatively, sections of the set can be assembled on wheeled platforms (trucks) for easier movement. On big opera stages there are often huge sliding platform-stages which can move a complete scene from the acting area into an off-stage dock.

Hemp flying

The simplest form of flying is hoisting scenery into the fly tower by sheer brute force—manual heaving on ropes without any assistance from machinery, counterweights or pulley systems giving mechanical advantage. This simple form of flying is usually known as *hemp* and a theatre equipped in this way is referred to as a *hemp house*—the word hemp indicating the ideal type of rope. The work is done from a gallery at the side of the stage known as the *fly floor* from which the ropes pass up to the *grid* (a supporting frame for pulley blocks at the top of the fly tower) and down to the stage. Each set of flying ropes consists of three lines, the *long*, the *centre*, and the *short*, named with reference to distance from the fly gallery.

The ropes are tied off in the fly gallery to large wooden or metal cleats. There are normally two rows of these cleat rails: the

Hemp flying with some temporary assistance from a sandbag used as a counterbalance (students at the National Theatre School in Montreal).

bottom row for the lowered position of the scenery and the top row for the raised position. These positions are known as *deads*. The *bottom dead* of a cloth, for example, would be when the bottom of the cloth was absolutely straight and just, only just, touching the stage floor—that is, touching without the floor taking any of the cloth's weight, for that would result in creases. When deading, instructions are given to the fly men in terms of in (down) and out (up) on the short, centre and long: for example 'in on your short, out on your long'. The lines are kept tied off on the bottom dead cleat and when the scenery is flown out of sight it is tied off on the *top dead*. Any piece of scenery flown as high as possible is said to be *gridded*. Sets of lines not in use are tied to a sandbag to provide weight for lowering to stage level when required.

Whereas gauzes, borders and light cloths can be handled in this way, the sheer weight of built scenery can make it difficult to fly smoothly. Moreover hemp flying is not just wasteful of manpower, it is rather unpleasant work. Mechanical assistance can be given to flying by rigging a pulley system with mechanical advantage—a billy-block—and this is particularly useful for the heaviest pieces. However, the real solution lies in counterweight flying.

Counterweight flying

Here the weight of the flown scenery is counterbalanced by an appropriate number of weights, usually iron but sometimes lead, in a cradle. Steel wires run from this cradle over grid pulleys to a metal bar (scaffolding or larger) running the width of the stage. A rope loop running from top of the cradle up to the grid, down to the stage floor and back to the bottom of the cradle allows one man to fly pieces of any weight in or out, provided that the correct number of weights have been added to the cradle. Ideally the cradle has the same travel as the bar and scenery which it is counterbalancing—that is, from grid to stage floor. The weight in the cradle will equal the weight to be flown. In some situations, particularly when there is restricted wall space due to the stage being much wider than the fly tower, or when there is restricted height above scene dock doors, all or some of the cradles can only travel half the distance of their fly bars. In these circumstances a system of double-purchase is used and the cradle carries twice the weight of the load.

Since the weights must be added to the cradle after the scenery has been attached, the weighting has to be done when the cradle is high (near the grid) corresponding to the bar being low (near the stage). Therefore there has to be a loading gallery just below grid level: while scenery is being hung a man must be positioned in this gallery to add weights to the cradles as necessary.

Safety in flying

Safety routines are very important in counterweight flying. Weights must not be added to the cradle until the scenery is attached to the bar and, conversely, scenery must not be removed from a bar until the counterweights have been removed. Otherwise the overweighted bar will run very fast to the grid. Counterweight systems have a lock which clamps on the handling rope and this should always be clamped when the set is not being handled. These locks, however, are not intended to hold a bar that is incorrectly weighted.

In hemp flying it is vital that no lines are untied from a cleat unless it is absolutely certain that enough men are standing by to

Counterweight flying.

take the weight.

In all flying, particularly during fit-ups, rehearsals and get-outs, it is essential that the flyman has a clear view of that part of the stage where the flown scenery will land or take-off. Where the flyman operating the lines cannot see, he should work under instructions from another flyman who can see.

Single purchase counterweights can be operated from a fly gallery or from stage level. Double purchase and hemp flying can only operate from a gallery. There are bonus points either way. At stage level the flyman may see more clearly and he is in better contact with other stage staff and stage management. In a fly gallery the atmosphere may be calmer and concentrated on one technical job; also it is easier to have advance warning of scenic pieces in the fly tower fouling one another.

Anything hanging above a stage must be regarded as a potential danger only to be averted by constant vigilance over such matters as knots, over-strained wires, etc.—not to mention hammers and other tools hooked 'temporarily' over a bar while working.

Advanced flying systems

Hydraulic and electric power has been applied to flying with two objectives: first, to simplify performances by allowing one-man operation of several bars moving at different speeds in different directions and, secondly, to simplify rigging by making the system self-balancing and thus free from the labour of manual counterweighting. The most elaborate of these systems is based on a series of single wire hoists which can be linked in any combination by a computer. It is a matter of concern to many experienced theatre technicians that some of the advanced flying systems now being installed do not include provision for manual operation if the machinery develops faults.

Flown scenery

Painted cloths, where the thickish paint would crack and crease if the cloth were folded, are normally fixed to timber battens at top and bottom by sandwiching the cloth between two pieces of wood. The cloth is stored and moved by rolling on its bottom batten. With hemp flying the ropes are tied directly to the top batten. With counterweights the batten is suspended from fly bar with chains. Dyed cloths and gauzes are usually supplied with tapes at top and a pocket at the bottom. The tapes can be tied directly on to the fly bar (or on to a timber batten in a hemp house) and the pocket can either be filled with chain or (probably better) a length of electrical type screwed conduit which will keep a gauze straight and stretched. This type of cloth is folded for storage. For ease in hanging all cloths and gauzes should have their centres clearly marked.

A *French flat* is a flown flat or series of flats battened together for flying. The weight must be taken from the bottom of the flat where a steel wire is attached to a *hanging iron* screwed or

bolted to the timber frame. This wire is kept flush to the flat by passing through a grommet at the top of the flat. The amount of wire between the top of the flat and the fly bar is known as the *drift* and care must be taken in calculation and measurement to ensure that it is not too short (the bar would come into sight) or too long (the flat would not fly completely out of sight). The portion of drift wire in sight is often painted black to avoid it glistening in the light.

Drapes or gauzes may be tied directly to the bar of a counterweight system (*left*). Battened cloths (*right*) are hung by chains.

Fly plots

All fly sets are numbered from downstage and are usually at fixed intervals of between six and nine inches (150 mm and 300 mm). In addition to the fixed numbering it is common practice to chalk the name of the flying piece (e.g. 'ballroom FF' or 'garden BC') on the frame adjacent to the cradle. Deads are marked on the ropes with coloured tape. Flymen usually keep two plots: a numerical list of all the hanging pieces and a running plot with the numbers of the bars that move on each cue.

Spot lines

When a single line is required for an effect, a lighting boom or perhaps to pick up something like the curved end of a cyclorama bar, a temporary *spot line* is dropped through the grid at the required position. If this line is to move on cue, it can be fed over pulleys to the fly gallery; if movement is not required, it is often tied off to fixings immediately above the grid.

The role of flying

Flying is a very useful way of storing and moving *two-*

dimensional scenery. It is the only way of handling cloths and it is a useful way of handling framed scenery provided that it sets parallel to the front of the stage. This is the main limitation of flying—it can only handle scenery in quantity if everything flies in one plane. It is possible to fly on the oblique but one flown flat set on an angle blocks all the lines between the upstage and downstage limits of that flat: the steeper the angle, the more lines blocked.

It is possible to fly flats parallel for storage, then set them on the oblique when they are at stage level, but it requires a tricky flying operation known as *overhauling*. After the scenery reaches the stage, the bar has to be lowered further until there is enough slack on the drift wires to allow the flat to be angled. To do this the flyman has to pull against the counterweights as they are no longer in counterbalance with the scenery. The technique has to be used with caution and is only advisable when the scenery is relatively lightweight and the scene change is not visible to the audience.

For changes carried out in sight of the audience, flying can be quick and graceful. For horizontal movements, curtains and gauzes can be flown on *tab tracks*: either the common overlapping twin track with a pair of tabs opening from the centre outwards, or a single *wipe* track where a single curtain can be drawn over all or part of the stage. Conventional tracks bunch from the onstage end of the track. *Rear-fold* tracks bunch at the

A Hanging Plot (*left*) lists the items suspended from each set of hemp lines or counterweight bar. The Fly Plot (*right*) records which items have to be flown in or out on each cue.

THEATRE ROYAL

HANGING PLOT   SHOW : "MERRY FLEAPIT"

40	ISORA
39	BALLROOM B.C.
38	GARDEN GAUZE
37	
36	ELECTRICS
35	ELECTRICS
34	
33	
32	PORTAL 3
31	GARDEN CUT
30	BALLROOM CUT
29	
28	ELECTRICS
27	
26	CONSERVATORY F.F.
25	BALLROOM CUT
24	KITCHEN BACKING
23	BLACK BORDER
22	CONSERVATORY CUT
21	
20	
19	KITCHEN F.F.
18	PORTAL 2
17	GARDEN CUT
16	LIBRARY CLOTH
15	BALLROOM CUT
14	
13	ELECTRICS
12	BLACK LEGS
11	KITCHEN F.F.
10	BLACKS
9	RUNNERS
8	SHOW CLOTH
7	GAUZE
6	
5	ELECTRICS (BAR)
4	ELECTRICS (BATTEN)
3	PORTAL 1 (SHOW PROS)
2	HOUSE BORDER
1	HOUSE TABS

THEATRE ROYAL

FLY PLOT

SHOW: "THE MERRY FLEAPIT"   ACT: I

CUE	MOVE	PRESET
		8, 17, 31, 38, 40
1	8 OUT	
2	7, 10 IN	17, 31, 38 OUT
3ₓ	10 OUT (BLACKS)	
4ˣ	7 OUT (GAUZE)	
5	22 IN	26 TO TOP DEAD UNTIL TRUCKS ARE SET.
6	8 IN	22, 26 OUT 19, 24 IN
7	8 OUT FAST	
8	7, 10 IN	19 + 24 OUT
9	7, 10 OUT	

off-stage and this can be a rather more elegant movement.

Generally speaking, counterweight flying is a very cost-effective way of handling scenery: once a piece is tied on to a bar and counterweighted it can be handled with ease, accuracy and certainty by one man.

Suspension on small stages

There are many proscenium stages without flytowers. Unfortunately many of these stages also have limited wing space or even none at all. If there is no flying space, there is often hanging space: material can be hung but not flown out. At worst there may be only a couple of feet and its use restricted to lighting equipment and masking borders. Cloths can be flown out of sight by *rolling*: the cloth is slowly lowered while a team roll it on the bottom batten after which the rolled cloth can be pulled out of sight. For rolling in sight of an audience it is posible to arrange lines to roll from the bottom on a special large diameter round timber.

With slightly more flying space available it is possible to *tumble* by raising the cloth on two sets of lines, one set from the top and one from the bottom. This way a cloth can be flown in half its height. To make the operation smooth, a round timber is often rolled in the fold.

The main hope for such a stage is to ensure that as many lines as possible are available. Minimum line and pulley provision is often made on the assumption that masking will be hung on *dead lines* tied from the top of a ladder. This is frustrating and time wasting.

The only true solution to the inadequate stage is to accept its limitations and adopt a scenic style that tries to make imaginative use of what exists, rather than try to adapt the technical facilities to do something for which they were never intended.

Built scenery

The aim of good scenery construction is to have a three-dimensional structure which can be assembled very quickly from two-dimensional components. If these component pieces are absolutely flat, they can be packed in a very tight wing space ready for assembly in a quick scene change. They will also take up minimum space in stores and transport trucks. The traditional *flat* is canvas stretched over a timber frame with every detail expressed in paint—including three-dimensional mouldings. With the growth of naturalistic styles in production, real mouldings have become an increasing feature of flat construction. Where these mouldings are relatively thin they are fixed permanently, but pieces of any considerable thickness should be provided with bolts to allow removal for transportation. The search for realism has led to flats being faced with plywood rather than canvas. While such flats may be fine for a permanent set, their weight complicates any scene change by requiring more staff and more time.

Flats supported by adjustable braces (*above left*) and French braces (*above*).

Flats packed against the scene dock wall (*left*).

The traditional method of joining flats is by line and cleat: the join is quick to make and, just as important, is quick to break. Heavier timber flats, or canvas flats top-heavy with cornices, etc., are often pin-hinged together. This method is firm and positive but it is in no way quick.

A well-designed and well-constructed set should almost stand up by mutual support, especially on a stage without a rake. Normally the flats will join at an angle and in an endeavour to give an impression of solidity there are likely to be quite a few pillars made from narrow flats meeting at right-angles. Where necessary, support is given by *braces*. Either the standard adjustable-length brace hooked into a screw eye on the flat and weighted or screwed into the floor; or the *French brace* hinged to the flat and weighted to the stage.

Contemporary scene design makes very little use of the technique of scene changing by building complete sets from flats. Standing box-sets of realistic rooms are still built from flattage but if a scene change is required, a more representational scenic style is likely to be adopted. The ever increasing weight of materials used in scene design and the need to reduce labour costs, together with the desire to let scenes flow continuously into one another rather than be broken by waits, has encouraged techniques of flying and trucking rather than manhandling. As a result, recent years have seen an increase in the amount of heavy handling involved in the setting-up preparations for a performance but a reduction in such handling during the performance.

Trucking

A lot of scenery is now mounted on castored platforms called trucks. Although a small scene may be mounted on a single

Joining by line and cleat (*below*); positioning rostra (*left*).

truck, it is common to have several trucks used rather in the nature of sub-assemblies. These are small enough to be stored in restricted wing space but relatively quick to push into position on the stage. The individual scenic elements usually pin-hinge to each other and to the truck base: the result is quite solid and rigid. Wherever possible the individual bits are flat for transportation.

False stages

When trucks are required to move 'magically' in sight of the audience without too obvious visible means of propulsion, it is possible to tack temporary slender timber guiding strips to the stage floor and manoeuvre the trucks with men concealed behind them or with lines or rods manipulated from the wings. Floor guides make life difficult for actors, especially dancers. For complex productions, like big musicals, a false stage floor is laid. This has tracks cut into it to guide the trucks, which are pulled to and fro by steel wire cables laid in the cavity between the original and false stage floors. Movement is normally by hand winches but motors are occasionally used.

Revolves

Revolving turntables may be built into the stage floor as part of the permanent equipment, or laid on top of the stage as part of the production's fit-up. The temporary revolve is the most adaptable as it can be made the appropriate size for the production. Drive is normally by hand winch for temporary revolves and by motor for permanent equipment. Revolves can be used to shift scenery with the curtain down or in a blackout but they are more interesting when used as a means of keeping

A small scene mounted on a truck to simplify setting and striking.

the production flowing from scene to scene while the actors continue the action. Apart from the conventional single revolve, twin revolves side-by-side have been used to good effect, particularly in musicals—each revolve changing the scenery on its own half of the stage.

Revolving stage designed for quick assembly (Ziller Technik).

Mechanised stages

In some parts of the world, mainly in Central European countries with a long tradition of repertoire opera, stages have extensive machinery installations. The main stage area is broken up into a series of elevator sections which can sink below the stage or rise above it. In some cases the understage area is so deep that entire scenes can be set below and brought up to stage level. Wagon stages are very common: there are various forms but perhaps the most frequently used is the cruciform: there are three wagons (left, right, and centre) which are the same size as the main stage's acting area. These wagons, carrying complete scenes, can be driven on to the main stage as required. In the off-stage position, large sound proof shutters allow scene changes to take place on the wagons while the performance continues. There are many variations of the engineered stage including enormous revolves of diameter much wider than the proscenium opening and with huge scenic lifts built in.

Studio stages

At the other end of the scale are the performances staged with planks and passion. Some studio stages are quite elaborately adaptable while others are a bare room (usually, but not necessarily, with some form of audience seating) to enclose actor and audience. There is only one desirable common structural factor for all studios: standard scaffolding bar diameter at strategic points on ceiling and walls to provide a universal fixing.

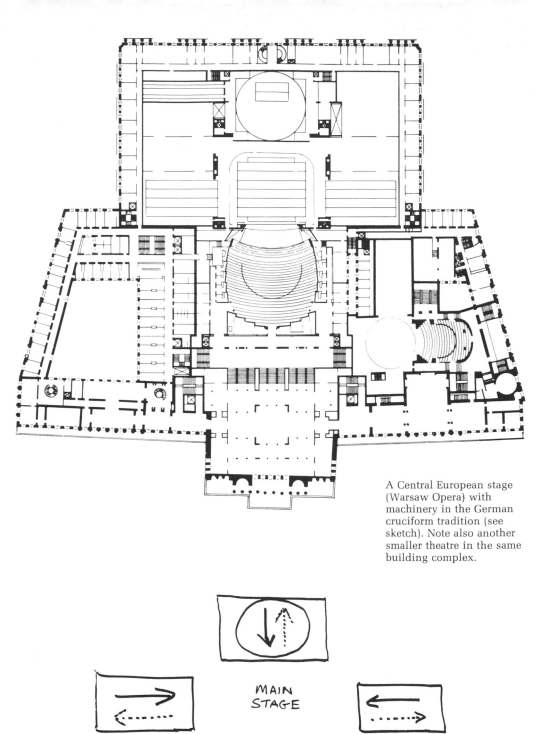

A Central European stage (Warsaw Opera) with machinery in the German cruciform tradition (see sketch). Note also another smaller theatre in the same building complex.

MAIN
STAGE

PROSCENIUM

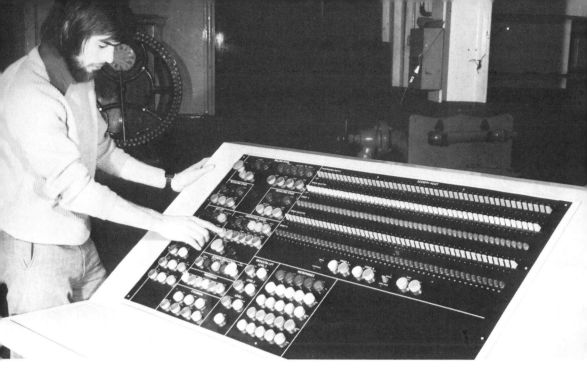

Materials

There seems to be no limitation on the type of material used in today's stage decor. This is partly a result of the search for new *textures* and partly because a representational style of design requires the representative objects to have what can only be called 'truth'. Certainly there seems to be a move towards less fake and less illusion.

In practical terms this means that scenery has become heavier. The tendency of flats to be covered in plywood rather than canvas has already been mentioned. Large chunks of metal, sometimes tortured to produce a textured surface, have become popular; as have structures built of expanded-metal shapes. GRP (glass reinforced plastic, often called 'fibreglass') and similar modern synthetics can be lighter to handle but the roughened textures which are sympathetic to light can be brutal to the hands. Foam plastics are very easy to work: indeed they are so easy that they need a considerable gauze appliqué to stop them crumbling at the edges.

Decisions about materials for cloths, gauzes and borders are closely linked with lighting.

Fireproofing

A major restriction on choice of material is fire risk. Actual regulations vary from country to country and in Britain the finer points are subject to the interpretation of the fire prevention officer within whose jurisdication a particular theatre is situ-

This control desk (manufactured by GEC Industrial Controls) for the stage machinery gives centralised control of the motorised movements of the stage wagons, revolves, lifts, proscenium opening, and flying.

A studio theatre.

ated. In judging borderline cases the fire officer usually takes into account his personal assessment of the local stage staff, particularly the resident stage manager. This makes a lot of sense since fire prevention owes a great deal to the sort of careful responsible attitudes that go beyond the chapter and verse of regulations.

Restrictions on materials are naturally more stringent in open stage theatres or on apron stages thrusting beyond the fire curtain. In conventional theatres, the proscenium wall is a fire-wall in which every opening has a steel fire-door so that once the fire curtain has been lowered a combination of fire-wall, smoke lantern and sprinklers will retard the spread of the fire until the auditorium has been evacuated.

Fire resistance is either an intrinsic property of a material (often by producing a self-extinguishing gas on burning) or superimposed by surface application of a chemical. Whenever possible, theatres buy ready fireproofed materials for scenic construction. Non-fireproof materials can be treated with fire-proofing solutions or fire-retarding paints. The fireproofing of fabrics, particularly gauzes, tends to wear off with time. Long running fabrics should be checked from time to time with a match (if you don't do it, the fire officer certainly will) and resprayed if necessary.

Painting

The art and craft of pictorial scene painting is in decline due to lack of demand. The pictorial style has been so unfashionable in

recent years that it is becoming quite difficult to find painters with the training and experience to realise a design incorporating 'traditional' perspective cloths, gauzes and borders. The role of paint in most of today's design styles is mainly textural, and developments in synthetic paints have simplified some of the problems of dealing with newer materials.

Projected scenery

Projection should not be regarded as a cheap and easy alternative to painted scenery. Full scale projection is complex and expensive: it is a technique to be used when the visual style of the production requires frequent and rapid changes of location and a translucent atmosphere. Most European operatic stages have full projection equipment as part of their permanent installation with the projectors located on properly positioned galleries. With few exceptions, projection in the rest of the world means a temporary installation of expensive equipment and problems arising from lack of depth on a shallow stage. Anyone tempted by projection should budget early and schedule extra time for pre-planning and for technical rehearsals. On the small stage, images from 35 mm slide projectors of the carousel type can be an interesting component of non-realistic design.

Models

The basis of any scenic design is the model and the ground plan, both normally on the scale of half-inch to the foot (metricated as 1:25). From these at least one section (on the centre line) is required in order to work out the hanging, including masking of lighting, with accuracy. Two-dimensional sketches are useful accessories to indicate the atmosphere of particular scenes but

they are no substitute for models, plans and sections.

Most scenery is designed in model form.

Bauprobe

The 'Bauprobe' or 'build rehearsal' is a Central European institution that could perhaps have wider application in theatres producing their own shows. Once a design is close to being finalised, it is set up roughly on stage using substitute flats, rostra, cloths, furniture, etc. Two things come out of this. Firstly the director, designer and choreographer are able to move about the dimensioned mock-up set to find out if the spacing is as they require. Secondly, minor adjustments in dimensions to enable the use of items like stock rostra or elevators may be suggested and demonstrated. Such changes may not affect the design concept but may save a lot of money in both initial production costs and daily running costs. However, it is usually easier for the technical staff to 'sell' this sort of idea to most designers by practical demonstration rather than by paper discussion.

Scenery organisation

The organisation of the scenic department from fit-up through rehearsals and performance to get-out is discussed in later chapters on the different types of show. Meanwhile the usefulness of a trial set-up in the workshop should be mentioned. Space problems often make this impossible but if the set—or sections of it—can be assembled prior to the stage fit-up, a check can be made on details like positioning of cleats and hinges. And the director may be able to anticipate problems over matters like door and step sizes. It is surprising how frequently, despite detailed planning, one hears phrases like, 'Oh, I didn't know the door was going to hinge *down*stage'.

6 Props

The term *properties*, invariably shortened to *props*, covers three overlapping categories: the *furnishings* (from sofas to thrones, and altars to kitchen sinks), the *dressings* (from portraits to rubber plants, and tapestries to plaster alsatians) and the *hand props* (from swords to martinis, and scrolls to telegrams). In all categories there are two kinds of props: *practical props* and the rest. Practical props behave like the real article although they are not necessarily real. For example, food that does not have to be eaten could be made from plastic, plaster or papier maché. Practical grapes for eating would probably have to be the real thing but the practical 'oyster' in an oyster shell could be but half a teaspoonful of clear jelly.

A prop design by Anna Welbourne for Hadrian VII.

Designing

The visual correctness of all props, whether specially made or not, is the designer's responsibility. Before rehearsals commence there will be a detailed prop list, but it is in the very nature of the rehearsal process that prop requirements, especially hand props, will change as the rehearsals proceed. Items will be added, cut and amended and the stage management must maintain day-to-day liaison with the designer.

Props can be made, bought, hired or borrowed. Some props are so specialised that they can only be made. Others may be available off the shelf either in ordinary shops or from specialist dealers. Whether such items are made, bought or hired is a budgeting decision taking into account not just relative initial cost but length of run, time and resources available for making, etc.

Making

The designs for large props to be made in the workshop should

HADRIAN VII
Processional Cross.

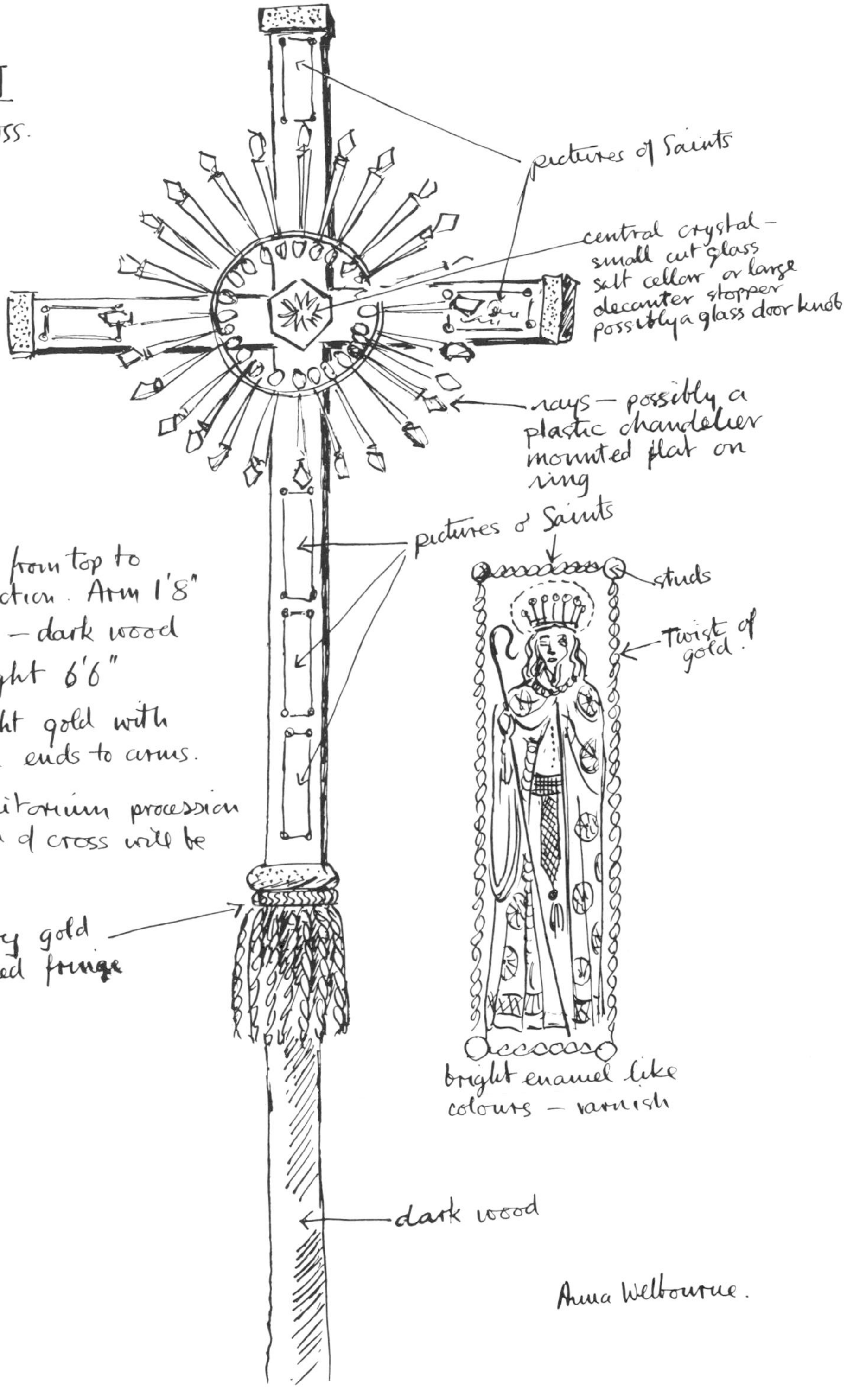

pictures of Saints

central crystal –
small cut glass
salt cellar or large
decanter stopper
possibly a glass door knob

rays – possibly a
plastic chandelier
mounted flat on
ring

pictures of Saints

studs

Twist of
gold.

Cross   2'9" from top to
     pole junction. Arm 1'8"
Pole 3'9" – dark wood
Overall hight 6'6"

Cross bright gold with
    textured ends to arms.

Note – Auditorium procession
   so back of cross will be
   seen.

heavy gold.
or red fringe

bright enamel like
colours – varnish

dark wood

Anna Welbourne.

be in model form but sketches, supplemented by discussion, are usually sufficient for smaller items. If a prop is practical, additional discussion is often required between propmaker and stage manager, possibly also director. In the case of comedians' props, direct discussion between propmaker and actor is essential. Many comics' laughs come from the manipulation of props and the simplest detail on the simplest prop is often quite crucial to success.

Buying and hiring

Buying and hiring of props is often delegated to junior members of the stage management. The designer will always choose furniture and wherever possible other major items should also be a direct designer choice. Any other members of the production team selecting items should reach an understanding with the shop that the item will be taken back against a refund if returned unharmed in, say, 48 hours. Prop buyers should bear in mind an old rule of thumb: weekly hire charge multiplied by length of run should not exceed cost of buying minus a pessimistic estimate of resale value. Fine for fixed runs but a bit tricky for speculative productions on Broadway or in the West End! In deciding whether to buy or hire, remember also that bought items may be modified and broken down with paint sprays whereas hired items must be returned 'as was'. Some items may only be available for hire: if it is a long run and there is no time to make, it may be worthwhile opening with a hired prop and making a copy later. The hire contract for props should include an agreed valuation for insurance.

Borrowing

Borrowing (i.e. hiring without payment) is only possible for very short runs. As the lender is doing a favour, a certain amount of tact is advisable on the part of the borrower. Lenders have been known to regard the action of borrowing an item but failing to use it as an affront to the lender's personal taste! So, sound a bit vague when borrowing—mutter something about 'production not finalised', etc. And don't forget to include borrowed items in the insurance.

Discounts, credits and comps

Some props, especially proprietary items, may be obtained at a discount or even free if a programme credit is offered. If this is agreed, it is important to be absolutely meticulous about the insertion of credits and their wording. Always send a copy of the programme to your contact in the firm giving discount. Complimentary tickets are often used to lubricate the prop department's relations with supplying firms: especially with members of firms who go out of their way to be helpful beyond the limits of strictly commercial duty.

Returns

A *returns list* of all hired and borrowed items should be filed with delivery notes and correspondence: this list to include not just addresses but the name of the 'contact' person in each firm. After the opening performance there are usually some discarded items to return and, of course, after the final performance all items should be returned immediately.

Rehearsal props

Props are required very early in rehearsals—often before they are ready. Substitute *rehearsal props* are therefore used and they should be as near to the actual props as possible. In cases where there is doubt about the size or shape of a prop, a rehearsal prop or series of alternatives is a useful way of finding out the actual requirement by a process of trial and error. Rehearsal props should be gradually replaced by the real props as they become available so that, by the final run-throughs in rehearsal room, the actors are using the same hand props as in performance. This removes another variable from the technical and dress rehearsals, thus allowing concentration on problems which cannot be solved in the rehearsal room.

A prop room.

Organising the props

Because there is usually such a large number of assorted items, props probably call for more organisation (checking, double-checking and re-checking) than any other staging department. The basis of organisation is plots, and prop plots fall into two categories: check plots and running plots.

Check plots

A check plot for any given time during the show will list the position of every single prop whether set on-stage, standing-by in the wings, or in the possession of an actor. Where props must be set in a special way, the check plot will include a drawing to show these positions. There will always be a check plot for the prop situation at the beginning of the show, and if there is any considerable movement of props, then there will be further check plots for certain points in the progress of the action, particularly interval breaks.

Running plots

Running plots show the prop *cues*. Some of these cues are props to be *set* (placed in position on the stage) or *struck* (removed from the stage) during a scene change. Other prop cues are handing props to actors before making an entrance and collecting props from actors after making an exit. In a scene change with a lot of props to be struck and set, the plot will list the actions of each individual member of the prop staff. These

Prop check plot (*left*) and prop running plot (*right*).

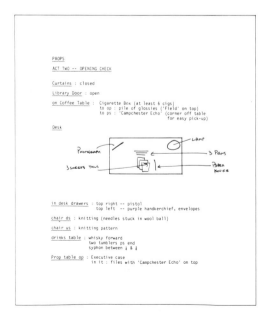

actions must be integrated so that props are changed in the correct sequence. Quite frequently the changing of the scenery cannot commence until certain props, often fragile, have been struck. Sometimes all the furniture can be moved quickly downstage to clear the scene and then taken off. Whenever possible, prop staff avoid double journeys by trying to set and strike at the same time.

Prop rooms

Many theatres have a prop room opening directly on to the stage. In addition to providing storage for smaller props, such a room usually has a bench and tools for minor repairs, and facilities (water, sink, cooker, etc.) for preparing prop meals and washing crockery. In theatres with limited facilities the prop room tends to double, unofficially, as a staff green room: this custom, pleasant though it is, should be resisted.

Prop trolleys

In some repertoire theatres, particularly in Central Europe, the props for each production are kept on wheeled storage trolleys so that the appropriate show can be brought quickly to the stage each day.

Prop tables

When there are lots of hand props, it is useful to lay them out on prop tables in the wings if space is available. The 'propiest'   Prop table.

shows are often naturalistic box set plays in which there can be so many actors' entrances with props that there has to be a prop table outside every door. For long runs, check plots can be pinned to the table and it is not unknown for the table to be marked off with labelled sections for each prop to give an at-a-glance check.

Personal props

The personal props that actors carry in their pockets need particular care since they are often handed to other actors or left on the set during the action. Most actors like to keep personal props in their dressing rooms and part of the pre-performance check is to make sure that all the necessary bits and pieces are definitely in the dressing rooms. Prop staff often enlist the aid of the actors' dressers in returning props to the correct dressing rooms.

Replacement props

If props have to be replaced due to breakages or wearing out during the run, tell the actors and show them the new prop if it is in any way different. Actors in a long run have been known to 'dry' completely on their first entrance when faced with the sight of a new carpet!

7 Lighting

Lighting is perhaps the most fundamental of all the stage techniques, for there is not much point in the actors doing their stuff if the audience cannot see them. With controlled light the attention of the audience can be focused on the appropriate part of the stage, and the actor can be clothed in an environment where the atmosphere is fluid but under precise control. For some considerable time lighting has been the growth area in theatre technology and, although sound is now leading the development field, an apparent air of glamour still surrounds the mysteries of the art and craft of stage lighting.

It is the craft rather than the art that we are concerned with here: the realisation of the conception rather than the conception itself. Art and craft are not, of course, separate little boxes. The art puts continual pressure on the craft to find ways and means of turning new ideas into reality, and the art is constantly stimulated by the craft possibilities of newly developed technology.

But the hard truth is that there is no point in having the most marvellous idea if that idea cannot be realised because there is neither the technology nor the time available. *Time* is the biggest problem in lighting. No matter how well the light has been pictured in imagination and planned on paper, it takes a long time to rig spotlights, focus them on the desired parts of the scene, and balance the appropriate combination for each cue in the lighting plot. Although rigging can be carried out while the scenery is being assembled, focusing and plotting can only be done satisfactorily once the scenic fit-up is complete. Being the last item in the staging schedule prior to the technical rehearsals with actors, the lighting rehearsal is under pressure to make up any time lost prior to this point. Consequently, to make the greatest possible creative use of this critical (one is tempted to say *most* critical) phase of the staging, particularly detailed advance planning is an absolute must.

Lighting designer

The person responsible for lighting planning is the lighting designer. This job can be doubled with director, designer, stage manager or chief electrician, but in most productions there is quite enough work involved to keep one person fully employed on lighting design alone. If the job is doubled, then the person taking on the additional responsibility for lighting design must understand the full extent of the pre-planning required.

The lighting designer has to be not only a mixture of artist and craftsman, he has to be a good chairman as well. Lighting is not superimposed but distilled from the ideas of author, director, designer and choreographer as well as lighting designer. There is often a considerable degree of compromise involved and it is the lighting designer who must resolve any conflicts of opinion among the production team, and evolve an acceptable unified concept that is capable of execution with the resources available.

Lighting equipment

Before considering lighting procedure, we should take a brief look at the tools of the lighting trade—the luminaires and control systems.

Floods
All luminaires (often called lanterns or instruments) consist of a lamp and optical system contained in a box with pivoting devices to allow pointing in any direction by means of a combination of two movements: up-and-down in a vertical axis (*tilting*) and side-to-side in a horizontal axis (*panning*). Where the light leaves the box, there are grooves to take a framed colour filter. The simplest form is the *flood* where the optical system is a fixed reflector. There are no adjustments other than tilt and pan so there is no possibility of adjusting the size of area lit other than by altering the distance between the flood and the area that it is pointing at. Floods are only useful for lighting large scenic areas like cycloramas and cloths. The lack of control over beam size and shape makes the flood unsuitable for lighting actors.

A lighting *batten* is a long compartmented trough extending

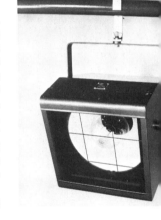

Flood (*above*)
Batten (*left*)

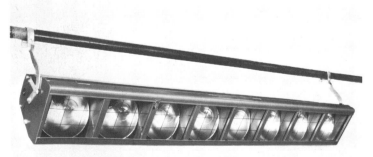

the width of the stage. Each compartment is really a small flood with the lamps wired in sequence to give either two, three or four colour mixing. Like single floods, battens are used for lighting scenery not actors; and their usefulness is restricted to large areas of canvas cloths and borders rather than the newer scenic techniques. For ease in handling, battens are usually manufactured in six foot sections. When placed at the front of the stage they are known as *footlights* or *floats* and when positioned anywhere else on the stage floor they are an *electrics groundrow*.

Focus Spot

Focus spots

The simplest form of spotlight has a lamp and reflector which together move backwards and forwards in relation to a fixed plano-convex lens giving control of the beam size. Simple focus spots are no longer used in Anglo-American lighting practice and British manufacture ceased more than twenty years ago. They are still used in Central Europe but there is every indication that their days are numbered.

Fresnel spots

In a fresnel spotlight, the lamp and reflector move in relation to a fixed fresnel lens which has a stepped front and mottled back giving a characteristic soft-edged quality to the light. A by-product of the soft-edged lens is a certain amount of stray light scattered outside the main beam and this can be distracting on scenery (especially masking borders or wings) adjacent to the spotlight. This scatter can be reduced and some control of beam *shape* gained by fitting a four-door rotatable *barndoor* shutter to the front of the fresnel lantern.

Fresnel Spot

Profile spots

The profile spotlight gives accurate control of beam *size*, *shape and quality*. The lamp and reflector are stationary: movement of the lens adjusts the quality of the beam edge to the required degree of hardness or softness. Size and shape of the beam are controlled at the optical centre of the system where there is a set of four shutters to provide any desired size of four-sided shape with straight edges. Adjacent to these shutters there is a slot (known as the 'gate') where an adjustable iris diaphragm may be inserted to produce circular beams of the required size. Alternatively a purpose-made mask (known as a *gobo*) may be used for specialised shaping. This type of spotlight is called 'profile' because it projects a profiled image of whatever shape is placed at the gate. The sophisticated reflector which surrounds the lamp is often ellipsoidal and so profile spots are sometimes known as *ellipsoidals*, especially in America.

Some profile spots have two sets of shutters: one set at the optical centre of the lantern is intended to produce hard edges while a second set, serrated and positioned a little way from the optical centre, gives soft edges. This allows hard or soft edges, or a mixture of hard and soft, to be produced quickly with a minimum of lens adjustment.

Profile Spot

Variable beam profile spots

In the latest types of profile spotlights, beam size and edge quality are controlled by differential movement of a pair of lenses. The shutters are then used only for shaping. By using this system (sometimes called non-coupled zoom) a wider range of beam angles is available from a single lantern. This makes them particularly suitable for repertoire and multi-use stages.

Beam lights

All the lens spotlights described above produce a conical beam and therefore the spread of light increases with the throw distance. The beamlight family have no lenses but the parabolic shape of their special reflector produces a parallel beam which lights the same size of area whatever the throw.

Variable Beam Profile Spot

PAR lamps have, built into the lamp's design, a disposable optical system giving a near-parallel beam. Used in a simple lantern with only pan and tilt adjustments for direction, these PAR lamps make useful members of the beamlight family, particularly when several are used together for a broad effect.

Follow spots

Spotlights which an operator uses to follow an actor around the stage are normally high-powered profile spots with sophisticated pan and tilt mountings for smooth movement. Until fairly recently the high light output was derived from a carbon arc but special discharge lamps (known as CSI or HMI) have now become standard.

Scene projectors

The CSI and HMI discharge lamps are opening up new horizons in scene projection, where the problem with conventional 5 kW

PAR Lamp Beamlight

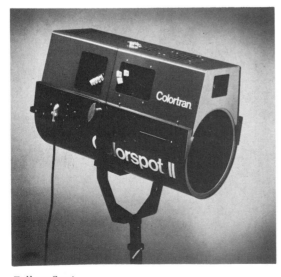

Follow Spot

Scene Projector.

and even 10 kW tungsten lamps has been to get enough brightness. All projectors require complex condenser lens systems, high quality objective lenses and forced cooling. Good equipment is therefore very, very expensive. Projectors for moving effects discs can use much lower quality optics and have much less power. Much projection work, especially in smaller theatres, is done with standard 35 mm magazine slide projectors of the carousel type.

Tungsten halogen

Newer spotlights, and conversions of some older ones, use tungsten halogen lamps. These lamps have a longer life and are a little brighter than the old tungsten lamps; but probably their most important feature is that they maintain full brightness throughout life. There is no gradual loss of light due to blackening of the glass.

Control systems

The central control point for the stage lighting is usually referred to as the *board*. This is a contraction of 'switchboard' and dates from the time when the stage lighting was worked from a massively engineered frame of switches and dimmer handles on a platform in the wings. The handles directly operated mechanical dimmers, which were normally resistances, although they were sometimes transformers in the more expensive models. After several interim experiments in miniaturising the boards so that they could be positioned to give the operator a view of the stage, the 1960s brought an electronic revolution to control systems. Some of the old direct-operated boards and some of the interims are still around but they are fast disappearing as spares and maintenance become difficult: it is an area in which the theatre archaeologist can have a field day.

Modern remote lighting control desk in auditorium control room with view of the stage (Rank Strand Compact Memory System).

Old type control (situated backstage).

All modern systems are two-part: the dimmers and the desk, linked by slender low voltage control lines. The dimmer room is the distribution point for electricity to the various sockets positioned around the theatre for feeding lights. The modern dimmer is almost universally a device called a *thyristor* and there is likely to be any number of dimmer channels from 6 to 240. It is difficult to do much with less than 6 and it is unusual to need more than 240: where a larger number is installed, it is usually to cover the total needs of a repertoire season where not more than a couple of hundred are likely to be used in a single performance. Most thyristor dimmers are designed to cope with any load between 40 w and 2 kW although most installations include a handful capable of dealing with up to 5 kW. The dimmer room is situated in any convenient back-stage position and the desk in an auditorium control room with a clear view of the stage. This is not just an ideal; it is standard practice in virtually all new theatres and in older theatres as they are refurbished.

The desks allow the levels for several lighting states to be preset in advance, then brought into play by operating master faders on cue. In European practice three or four presets are standard but in America up to ten presets are common. Consequently the presets have to be reset many times during the sequence of any show with more than the very smallest number of cues. To get round this, the data storage techniques of computer technology have been applied to lighting control and the new *memory boards* (as the jargon has it) store the levels for a virtually limitless number of lighting states. The actual memory capacity naturally depends on cost but around 200 memorised cue-states in the main memory is quite common. A cassette tape acting as a secondary memory to feed information to the main memory can extend the range towards infinity.

Since many of the components are by-products of other technologies, the growth of memorised lighting control in the theatre since the early 1970s has been quite staggering. What was regarded as luxury a very few years ago has now become commonplace. Memory boards may soon become standard for any installation of more than 30 (perhaps even 20) circuits.

Lighting procedure

Although the lights and the control desk are the obvious tools of lighting design, there is another piece of equipment which is just as important: the *drawing board*. After script study and discussions to formulate a mutually agreed answer to the question 'What is light doing for us in this production?', the lighting designer must decide:

> Where to put the lights
> Which lights to put
> Where to point these lights
> Which colours in which lights

These decisions are made at the drawing board. How they are made is not the subject of this book. Our concern is with organisation: what decisions are required, how they are communicated to the other staging departments, how they are integrated with the decisions of these departments, and how they are implemented during the staging period in the theatre. With these procedures in mind, let us follow through the planning and implementation of the lighting design.

Plans

The basic document of lighting design is the lighting layout plan. It has two functions: the action of drawing is the means of working towards the decisions, and the completed drawing is the means of communicating these decisions. The basis of the lighting plan is the designer's ground plan, normally drawn to a scale of 1:25. The lighting designer works by pinning a sheet of tracing paper to this ground plan and drawing his equipment in position, using symbols to indicate the various types of lighting instrument. The easiest symbols to use (and subsequently the easier to read) are scale stencils of the various manufacturers' lantern shapes.

At the drawing board, the eraser is as important as the pencil. The first attempt nearly always uses too many lanterns: too many for the money budgeted, too many for the time scheduled and very probably too many for the lighting to have a clean positive quality. A substantial part of the design process is refining down—examining the role of every spotlight to see if it is really essential, often by asking the question, 'What would happen if we did not have this light?' This elimination process usually results in a more practical rig and a cleaner visual effect.

The completed plan shows the types of lantern, their positions, their colours, and their control-channel numbers. The usual convention is to put the colour filter numbers inside the lantern symbol and the channel number alongside. A note is made beside the lantern of any special accessories such as gobo, iris, barndoor etc. After drawing all the lighting, enough detail of the scenery ground plan is traced through to indicate the geographical relationship between lighting equipment and scenery.

The aim of an ideal plan is that it should include enough information for the rigging electricians, without the lighting designer being present, to get every lantern hung in the correct position, with the correct colour and accessories, and fed from the correct dimmer. The lighting designer should be able to walk in at the conclusion of rigging, find no surprises, and start focusing immediately. In practice, a wise lighting designer will try to visit or telephone during the rigging: no matter how immaculate the plan, unforeseen circumstances (often in the shape of revised scenery hangings) may produce a rigging problem requiring revision.

To communicate his intentions to the rest of the production team, the lighting designer should circulate copies of the plan to designer, production manager, production carpenter and stage management, in addition to the electrics staff. To keep the plan as simple to read as possible, detailed focus information is not normally included on these copies of the plan. It is pencilled on the lighting designer's copy and amended while he watches run-throughs in the rehearsal room. Indeed one of the problems of lighting plans is that they have to be drawn—so that equipment can be ordered and things like colours and cables prepared—before the production takes final shape in rehearsal. This is just something that has to be lived with, remembering that it is easier to alter a plan than to have no plan at all.

Sections

During his design work at the drawing board, the lighting

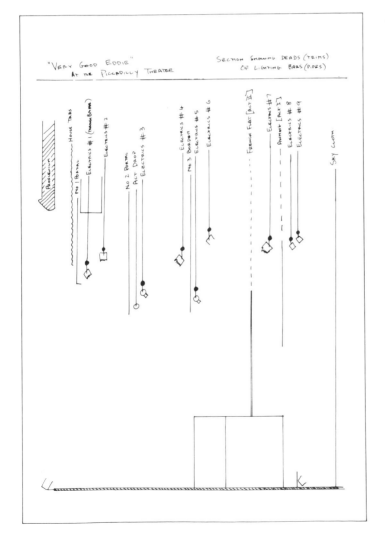

A lighting design section.

designer requires a sectional drawing. For a proscenium show where the flying runs parallel to the setting line, one section through the centre line is enough but for an asymmetric open stage setting, sections taken on several axes may be necessary. On the sectional drawing, the lighting designer can see the angles at which his lights will hit the actors. He can check the height required for his lighting bars to mask, and if the top and bottom deads of the flying scenery are shown, he can check whether the light beams will hit the required scenic pieces when they are flown in, without being obstructed by scenery which is flown out.

The finalised drawings used for rigging the stage production show all the lighting bars at their correct heights (i.e. their *deads*, or, to use the American term which is becoming universal, *trim*). Amazingly, some productions are still fitted-up without the help of a section on which all the deads, both scenic and lighting, have been decided. This saving of planning time leads inevitably to a waste of the infinitely more precious staging time.

Equipment schedules

From the plans, a detailed schedule of lighting requirements is prepared. This shows the numbers of each lantern required, plus listings of accessories and colour filters, and a dimensional breakdown of rigging into bars, booms, clamps, brackets and cabling.

Hire

If additional equipment is required to augment the theatre's stock, a list of hire requirements can be extracted from the equipment schedule. Lighting hire has become rather competitive and it is wise to seek quotations from at least a couple of rental companies. In comparing quotes, the companies' relative reputations for service should be taken into account: the cheap-to-rent lantern requiring cleaning, maintenance and adjustment during rigging and focusing could turn out to be a rather expensive saving.

Cue synopsis

The lighting designer pops into the rehearsal room from time to time to see how the production is taking shape. From these visits, particularly to run-throughs towards the end of the rehearsal period, and from various discussions with the director and designer, the lighting designer begins to formulate a clearer and clearer picture of how it will all look. Immediately before the final technical and dress rehearsal period, the lighting must be broken down into specific cued changes. This list of lighting changes, the *cue synopsis*, gives the Q number, timing, position in script, and a short verbal description of each lighting change. This list should be prepared by a committee of the lighting

"VERY GOOD EDDIE"			Piccadilly Theatre
Page	**Cue**	**Time**	**Purpose**

TIME BETWEEN CUES (MINUTES)

NB: Floats on & house tabs in from opening of the house at the half.

Time between cues	Page	Cue	Time	Purpose
3	1	Q.1.	3sec	As Tabs out X-fade to act drop light
2	1	Q.2.	3sec	As act drop out : bright day
4	2	Q.3.	10sec	end of opening number : check upper level
2	5	Q.4.	8sec	preparing for number : small check
2	5	Q.5.	8sec	into "Some sort of Somebody" : check
3	5	Q.6.	8sec	restore to Q.2. state (end of number)
3	8	Q.7.	6sec	into "Size 13 collar" : biggish check
1½	10	Q.8.	8sec	restore (not upper level)
2	11	Q.9.	6sec	into "Bungalow". Warm (ie lose blues)
1½	12	Q.10.	5sec	restore (with upper level)
4	14	Q.11.	8sec	into "Happily Married" : small build
1	17	Q.12.	8sec	into "Good Night Boat" : biggish check
1	18	Q.13.	8sec	during number : more check
1	18	Q.14.	8sec	end of number : restore to Q.8. with mods.
2	20	Q.15.	5sec	into "Blues" : check, cool
6	21	Q.16.	6sec	restore @ end of number
2½	25	Q.17.	6sec	into "Hot Dogs". Build warms & check cools
1	26	Q.18.	15sec	end of number. restore to Q.16 state
2	27	Q.19.	6sec	into "Million in the Bank". re-balance to DS
4	27	Q.20.	5sec	restore
1	30	Q.21.	8sec	"Friend of mine" : check
1	30	Q.22.	8sec	Build for dance (especially booms)
1	31	Q.23.	8sec	Build (to about ¾ of available)
½	31	Q.24.	8sec	restore to Q.20 state
½	32	Q.25.	5sec	concentrate centre
1	32	Q.26.	5sec	restore to Q.24 plus
	33	Q.27.	3sec	house tabs in

designer, director, designer, and the member of the stage management who will 'run' the show and call the cues. If the choreographer and costume designer have a strong contribution to make to the discussion they will wish to be present; otherwise they will delegate their representation to director and scene designer respectively.

If pressure on time prevents this meeting, then the lighting designer should draw up his own proposed list and circulate it for comment. Either way, before the first lighting rehearsal, it is essential that the cues be pencilled into the prompt copy. The importance of this should be apparent in later chapters.

Rigging methods

Wherever possible, lighting instruments are fixed to horizontal or vertical alloy tubing with the external diameter of standard scaffolding ($1\frac{7}{8}$ in or 47 mm). Horizontals are known as *bars* (*pipes* in USA) and verticals as *booms*. Hook clamps and boom arms are designed to hang lanterns so that both lanterns and lamps operate on their correct axis for maximum lamp life. Brackets are useful for temporary rigging of single lamps, particularly those hung from the timbers of flats but their use is far too limiting for a permanent installation. In auditorium positions in particular, lengths of standard tubing give much more flexibility than brackets.

Rehearsing the lights

The integration of lighting rigging with the scenic fit-up is discussed in the section of the book dealing with the details of the staging process for various types of production.

Electrics postscript

Production lighting is not the only function of the electrics department. They provide lights for rehearsal pianos, production desks, music stands and quick-change rooms. They rig special cue lights and provide feeds for smoke guns. They deal with irons, washing machines, spinners, drying cabinets and all the other modern aids to wardrobe and wig maintenance. They cope with actors' shavers, portable television sets and hair-dryers. In all except the largest repertoire theatres, the production electricians double up as the building's maintenance staff. Allow for this in scheduling, and notify *all* foreseeable requirements in advance of the get-in.

8 Sound

Electronically processed sound is used in the theatre for three purposes: the *reinforcement* of the level of vocal and instrumental sound produced by the performers, the addition of sound *effects*, and for *communications*.

Sound reinforcement

Reinforcement of the level of sound is not just a matter of the degree of amplification, it is a positive component of production *style*. 'How are we going to use sound?' must be an early question in production planning. It is a question that should surface from time to time as the director and his team work out their conception of the production prior to the commencement of rehearsals. Theatre sound technology has advanced to the point where it is no longer something superimposed during the dress rehearsal. Sound is an integral part of a stage presentation and it requires *design*.

The decision may well be to use no form of sound reinforcement: fine, so long as it is a deliberate, conscious decision made only after consideration of the theatre's acoustics and the actors' projection ability. If the sound is to be reinforced, it can be done *sub-consciously*, *consciously* or as an *intrinsic* production technique.

Sub-conscious reinforcement

Audiences have become accustomed to higher sound levels than formerly. Home radio, television and records tend to be adjusted to levels sufficiently high to make concentration unnecessary for listening. Cinema has helped the process and the gradual introduction of more and more sound reinforcement into the theatre has brought the average audience to the point where they no longer expect to have to make any sort of active effort to hear.

The correct sound level is a vital component of the actor-audience relationship. To make contact the actor must be clearly heard, yet an excess volume of sound can act as a barrier. Perhaps the way to find the ideal level is to cut back to the point where the audience are on the point of having to concentrate. The threshold of concentration is considerably louder than the threshold of audibility!

Reinforcement is not normally required for speech in theatres which have been built specifically as playhouses. This includes the smaller auditoria of the old traditional theatre centres like Broadway and the London West End. It also includes the smaller, say up to about seven or even eight hundred seater, regional theatres built specifically for the spoken word in the last couple of decades. It does not include most of the large mixed-programme houses built fifty-plus years ago when touring was at its extensive height. And it does not include most of today's multi-purpose halls. For this situation some reinforcement is required but it should be as discreet as possible, so that the audience are not too consciously aware of it.

This means discreet positioning of microphones. In old horse-shoe theatres with a relatively narrow proscenium opening (certainly not more than 30 ft) it may be possible to use long range 'gun' microphones on the box fronts nearest to the stage, but normally a series of 'float mikes' along the front edge of the stage are required. The latest designs have small heads on slender columns so that they are relatively unobtrusive. Radio microphones concealed by the actor's clothing, although acceptable in the higher ambient noise circumstances of a musical show, are still too prone to miscellaneous rustlings and cracklings for the straight play. In any case, maintenance of a consistent sound quality would require every single actor, even the 'one-liners', to be individually miked. This is not possible in Britain at the present time due to the limited 'air space' made available by the authorities.

The discreet placement of microphones is not the only feature of subconscious reinforcement. The primary source must appear to be the actors rather than the loudspeakers. This obviously requires particularly high quality equipment and the use of a relatively low level of amplification. In this way some resemblance can be maintained of a logical relationship between level of sound and distance between speaker and listener.

Opera is possibly the one form of theatre that never needs reinforcement—with the possible exception of the continuo harpsichord when a chamber opera is played in a large house designed for romantic opera. However with louder and louder stereophony and quadrophony in the home, it could well come to pass that a future generation of opera-buffs might demand that their live opera performances be reinforced to reach the level which can be produced by a high gain record reproducer in a small room.

Conscious reinforcement
In musicals there is now very rarely any attempt to apply a

discreet reinforcement of which the audience will only aware at a subconscious level. Microphones are prominently in view and the sound is amplified to a level which it would be difficult to ignore. The same situation applies even more so in 'light entertainment', the modern descendant of the music hall and variety stages, where personality performers work directly to the audience. The microphone becomes a vital prop and its handling is a carefully rehearsed and essential part of the performer's technique. The use of the microphone can be made so much a conscious part of the production style that radio microphones are often handled as props rather than concealed in costumes.

Intrinsic reinforcement
For many forms of modern music, the studio recording rather than the written score has become the definitive form of publication. The music only exists when the individual vocal and instrumental threads have been electronically processed. The tempo and phrasing remain the responsibility of the conductor but his traditional control of balance has been handed over to the sound designer's mixing desk.

This approach is now applied to the writing of stage shows, particularly rock musicals, and indeed in some cases the record has appeared first, its success providing the stimulus for mounting a stage production. In such circumstances the theatre sound quality must obviously strive to match that of the studio recording. To do this the sound becomes an intrinsic part of the production with each vocal and instrumental part separately picked up by its own microphone and balanced through a multi-channel mixer of studio proportions. Actors' movements are adjusted to suit microphones rather than the other way round. Sound assumes a major role in the budget and has become so fundamental that it is probably no longer correct to talk of it as mere reinforcement.

Taped vocals
It is difficult to sing well while dancing an energetic choreographed chorus routine. One solution is to dance to a playback of tape-recorded song. To add to the realism, the dancers try to sing a bit rather than just mime and the orchestral accompaniment is live. The cueing of the tape at the start of each sequence requires critical timing and the usual method is for the musical director to have a remote start button on his music stand in the orchestra pit. As a precaution against breakdown, there is also a stand-by tape running in synchronisation with the main tape. Carefully used, the technique can be made to look plausible, but it suffers from a major drawback: the tape sets an inflexible timing and it is the subtle variations in timing that make a live show live.

Foldback
All the sound reinforcement discussed above has been for the benefit of the audience and the loudspeakers have been directed at them. In many circumstances, sound reinforcement has to be directed towards the actors from on-stage loudspeakers. This is

called *foldback* and is a separate mix from that fed to the audience. In opera, although there is no reinforcement for the audience, some foldback from the pit is often required to let singers hear their accompaniment and pick up note pitches. In reinforced shows (particularly those with conscious reinforcement) actors usually need foldback not only to hear their accompaniments but also to hear their own voices at a level high enough to give them confidence that they are being heard by the audience.

Audience reaction reinforcement
All the increase in performance sound levels can make the applause, laughter and general audience reaction 'buzz' seem quiet by comparison. This could be detrimental to that audience communal feeling which is an essential part of the actor-audience relationship. There is therefore a case for giving the audience some foldback of their own reactions. When this technique is used, it is done with considerable discretion because there are those who might consider the amplification of applause or laughter to be cheating.

Sound equipment

Mixers
The heart of the reinforcement installation is the *mixer* where the inputs from the various microphones are combined and routed to the appropriate loudspeakers. There is a parallel between the sound mixing desk and the lighting control desk in that both function by balancing the relative levels of the various input channels (indeed, 'light mixer' would probably be a more appropriate term than the customary 'lighting control' or 'dimmerboard' or 'switchboard').

The most important component in any sound channel is therefore the *fader* for controlling the level at which that channel's microphone contributes to the mix. In early mixers the fader was a rotary control ('pot') and it may still be in simple inexpensive models. In mixers of the standard desirable for professional theatre use, however, the fader is a linear slider which is easier to read—both at a glance and by feel. To allow the full travel of the fader to be used, there is often a channel *sensitivity* control which sets the maximum level of its channel. This spreads the available range of travel from zero to agreed maximum, across the whole length of the fader. By limiting the maximum level, that channel fader can be operated without risk of going into the high pitched squeal of howlround (often called 'feedback').

Unlike a lighting desk, a sound mixer desk controls quality as well as quantity. Each channel has *equalisation* controls to adjust the tonal quality. It is usual to find a minimum of three rotary pots for equalisation, giving cut or boost to the *treble*, *mid*, *and bass* frequency bands. So that the cut and boosted tonal quality can be compared with the original non-equalised sound, there should be an *equalisation cut* switch.

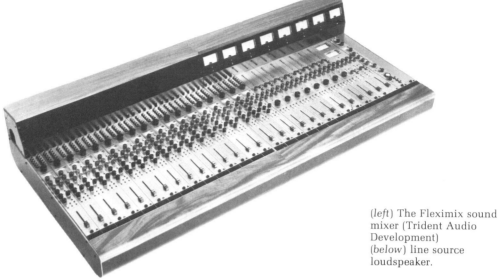

(*left*) The Fleximix sound mixer (Trident Audio Development)
(*below*) line source loudspeaker.

A *PFL* (*pre-fade-listen*) switch allows the operator to check in advance that the channel is working or an off-stage actor standing-by. Auxiliary controls are likely to include facilities for *foldback* (at a level either subject to the channel faders or independent of them) and facilities for introducing optional *echo* into the channel. Finally there are routing controls to allow the channels to be grouped with other channels under the overall control of master faders. The mixer feeds the power amplifiers and there are further controls to route the output to the appropriate loudspeakers.

With a big musical using upwards of forty channels, a mixer operator can have an awful lot of pots to control. Small wonder, therefore, that the possibility is being explored of applying memory facilities to some of the routine operations so that the operator's hands and mind are free to concentrate on the fader levels which require a subtle balancing that varies from one performance to another.

Microphones

There are two types of microphone in standard use for sound reinforcement in theatres: *dynamic* and *condenser*. Although dynamic microphones are more robust, the condenser types give the highest quality (and consequently are more expensive). They need more careful handling than the more robust dynamic types. Condenser mikes are often used for the main pick-up positions, particularly floats, with dynamic mikes in subsidiary positions.

Some microphones (sometimes called 'non-directional' but more properly *omni-directional*) are equally sensitive in picking up sound from all directions. Others are only sensitive in certain directions. One type, often known as *figure-of-eight*, is sensitive to the front and rear but insensitive to the sides. The most useful types for theatre are *cardioid* (directional) and *hyper-cardioid*

(very directional). These have heart shaped pick up patterns which are extremely sensitive to the front but virtually dead to the sides and rear. This enables the microphone to be 'focussed' on the desired part of the stage action and because the dead sides are towards the loudspeakers, there is a diminished risk of picking up the sound from the loudspeakers and so developing howlround. Some condenser mikes have variable directional qualities. The most directional pick-up is from gun microphones (sometimes called 'rifles') but, while they are undoubtedly very useful up to about three times the range of a normal cardioid, they are not miracle workers. They will not, as had to be proved to a director by demonstration recently, pick up the actors and ignore the orchestra when fixed to a balcony from some forty feet from stage and pit.

At the other extreme, microphones attached to the actor, whether hung around the neck on cords or clipped to the costume, have to be omni-directional. To allow freedom of movement these microphones usually feed their signal to a small radio transmitter.

In some theatres, particularly those used for variety, revue, pantomime and similar forms of light entertainment, *riser* microphones are fitted at the front of the stage. By remote control these can be raised through traps in the stage floor to the appropriate height required by the performer.

Loudspeakers

Whereas the microphone converts sound into electrical energy, the loudspeaker converts the electrical impulses back into sound—after they have been processed in the mixer and magnified in the power amplifiers. Just as the microphones have to be directional in picking up the actors, so too must the loudspeakers be directional in distributing the sound to the

The latest loudspeaker techniques, as in the BOSE system, allow an even distribution of the full frequency range from a compact enclosure.

Float microphones.

audience. A directional loudspeaker system not only directs the sound towards the audience, it ensures that the amplified sound is not fed back in any quantity to the stage where it would be picked up again by the microphones to produce howlround. What we commonly refer to as loudspeakers are in fact two-part: the actual loudspeaker units and their housings or cabinets for which the proper word is *enclosures*.

There are two kinds of loudspeakers used in theatre work: *line source* and *horn*. The *line source* has a column of separate cone loudspeakers mounted vertically in a long slender enclosure. The directional effect of doing this is to restrict the vertical coverage and increase the horizontal coverage of the sound. In the highest quality models there are separate columns of high and low frequency cones in the same enclosure. Mounted near the proscenium arch, they help maintain the illusion that the sound is coming from the stage. They can be angled so that they give a wide horizontal coverage of the audience yet do not blast the people in the front rows who will receive sound from only the lowest speakers in the column. These line source speakers are reasonably elegant and do not conflict unduly with theatre auditorium architecture. They are therefore useful for sub-conscious reinforcement.

As the sound becomes a more dominant feature of production style or the auditorium becomes particularly large, it is necessary to move into loudspeaker types which, although more physically obtrusive, have improved frequency response and power output. These use a combination of high frequency *horn* units and separate bass horns in chunky enclosures designed to enhance bass response.

Wiring
Microphones, mixers, amplifiers and loudspeakers have to be linked by wiring. The recent growth of sound has been so fast that much permanent wiring has become obsolescent almost as soon as installed. The very nature of an adaptable sound system implies considerable amounts of temporary wiring but with a good permanent installation, the temporary runs can be kept reasonably short. The whole process relies on a high quality standardised plug and socket interconnection system. This whole subject is beyond the scope of this book and we can only entreat anyone responsible for specifying sound wiring to 'think big' and to study appropriate recommendations—in Britain, for example, the sound wiring recommendations published by the Association of British Theatre Technicians are becoming standard practice.

Sound control position
In older theatres the termination point for microphone and speaker lines is usually adjacent to the prompt corner. In newer theatres the lines all go to jack fields in a sound control room forming part of the lighting, sound and projection suite at the rear of the auditorium. This sound control room usually contains effects tape decks and turntable in addition to the mixer. For

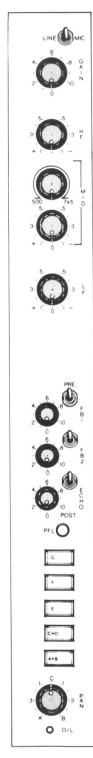

productions making any considerable use of reinforcement, however, there is a very very strong case for the mixer being in the auditorium so that the operator can balance live rather than through monitor loudspeakers.

Sound effects

Sound effects can be live, reinforced-live, or taped. The choice, once again, is largely a matter of production style.

Live effects
Over the centuries, prior to the arrival of electronically processed sound, the theatre has developed methods of producing realistic effects on cue. Coconut shells for horses' hooves is probably the effect that has most caught the public imagination and any sensitive theatre worker must have an occasional nostalgic yearning for the days when a storm could command an

A typical sound control channel (*opposite*). The associated fader would be mounted below, but at a different angle to make fingerwork easier. (*below*) A thunder run at Her Majesty's Theatre, London. Such effects are now reproduced from tape.

orchestra of wind machines, rain machines, drums ad lib and sinister rumblings from a series of cannonballs rolling through a permanent thunder run in the upper regions of the stage and possibly above the auditorium as well. Apart from any other considerations, such complex sequences are now usually ruled out by the large number of operators required. However, for simpler effects like door slams and glass crashes, the old live way is probably still the best.

Reinforced live effects
If the actors' voices are being reinforced, any live effects will probably require to be reinforced as well, partly to make them loud enough and partly to give them the same tonal quality as the voices. The effect is performed to a microphone and an appropriately positioned loudspeaker produces the sound from the logical direction.

Taped effects
Most sound effects are now inserted in the performance by replaying a specially edited tape. Reel-to-reel machines rather than cassettes are used, to simplify editing. Where possible, the effects are arranged in sequence on a single tape with short coloured leaders between each cue. On the older machines, metal foils are used to line up the next cue automatically but most decks now use clear tape and a photo cell.

If the sound plot is very complex there may be an overlap of various sounds, and this overlap may vary from night to night

The sound control room in the Sherman Theatre, Cardiff (equipment by Electrosonic).

due to the timing variations that are the inevitable and characteristic feature of a live stage performance. To cope with this, theatres normally use twin track machines. Different effects can be recorded on each track to be mixed as desired during replay. Many theatre installations include two twin-track machines and this gives enough flexibility for the average production. $7\frac{1}{2}$ inches per second is the standard speed used.

If a movement of sound from one part of the stage to another is required, the effect can be 'panned' (i.e. crossfaded) from one loudspeaker to another: this provides more precise control of the performance timing of the sound's movement than if it were recorded in stereo with a fixed timing.

Specific effects may be obtained from a sound library and/or they may be recorded specially. Recording of the 'real' sound seldom works: as in the case of live effects, a faked sound often has more realism. Specialist books on sound give some useful starting hints but one should allow time for recording experiments. Fortunately tape can be wiped and re-used.

Communications

Communications between technicians during performance are now carried out almost entirely by voice. In simple shows, cue lights may still be used to signal to the flymen and other backstage positions but voice is invariably used for electrics (dimmerboard and follow spots). Cue lights are still installed in these positions but are only intended for emergency use in the event of a breakdown in the sound network. The two basic methods of sound communication are by *talk-back* and *ring intercom*.

Talkback
The central command position is the stage manager's prompt desk where there are key switches to route his microphone to all or any of the important technical areas, such as lighting control, sound control, follow spots, flys, understage, lighting bridges, staff room etc. Outstations wishing to speak to the stage manager can signal by flashing lights on the desk and the SM will accept the call if he is free. Loudspeakers are useful for fit-ups and technical rehearsals but headsets are normally required for positions within the stage area during dress rehearsals and performances (lighting control is often a sound-proof room and the follow spot box may be also). In addition to the fixed microphone on the SM desk, there should be a socket for a roving microphone so that the stage manager has freedom to move temporarily away from the desk to positions where he can see the stage action appropriate for the giving of certain cues. New prompt desks are often portable so that they can be moved to the position most suitable for a particular production: a roving microphone facility is still necessary, however.

Ring intercom
For additional communication among technicians, it is now

standard to have a wiring loop linking all the technical areas. At key positions there are socket boxes into which a headset may be plugged to allow that position to talk and listen to everyone else using the loop. There is usually a button to flash a light on all boxes to attract the attention of any technician in the vicinity.

Inductive loops

It is possible to run a loop aerial around the building so that technicians can carry small radio receivers with ear-pieces of the deaf-aid type. Unfortunately the amount of steelwork in a modern theatre acts as a screen, making reception uncertain in important areas like bridges and understage. However, inductive loops are the standard method of relaying simultaneous translation of foreign language plays to individual members of the audience; and they have been used successfully to cue technicians driving trucked scenery with complex movements. In emergency, but only dire emergency, an inductive loop could be used for prompting.

Radio microphones

Radio microphones are useful for focussing lights. The lighting designer has to move all over the stage while calling channel numbers to the switchboard and giving instructions to electricians who may be on distant bridges. A radio microphone into the communication system gives freedom of movement and is particularly useful in repertoire theatres where refocusing of spotlights may be required during scene changes.

Production desk

Communication facilities are required for rehearsals at the production desk position in the auditorium. There should be access both to ring intercom and to the stage manager's talk-back. Priorities should be arranged in favour of the stage manager—that is, pressing the SM talk key should cut-out any other traffic. At dress rehearsals it is convenient for the lighting designer to hear the lighting cues over the talk-back and to use the system to talk to the lighting operator between cues, if necessary. At lighting rehearsals direct communication between lighting designer and control room is necessary and, as these sessions can be rather prolonged, it is useful if this does not involve wearing a headset ('cans' in jargon) but is a two-way microphone/loudspeaker system without switches (a 'hands-off' intercom in jargon). Provision should be made for the director to speak to the cast in a show of any size and this can be quite tricky to arrange in a musical without introducing howlround.

Dressing room calls

Dressing room loudspeakers are fed with two programmes: show relay and stage management calls. When calls are being given, the show relay is automatically cancelled. There is a knob on each speaker to adjust the volume of the show relay but this does not affect the calls. There is usually a subsidiary microphone in the stage door keeper's office but this is automatically overriden by the call key on the stage manager's microphone.

Telephones
In a theatre of any size there will be an internal administrative telephone network with key technical areas included. When these telephones are within sound of the stage or auditorium they should have a flashing light as an alternative to the normal bell.

Closed circuit television
In theatres where latecomers are prevented from taking their seats until a suitable pause, it is usual to relay the performance by closed circuit television. When this facility is available, it is useful to include a monitor in the prompt corner as an aid to stage management. In opera houses there is always a CCTV camera in the pit to relay the conductor's beat to the off-stage areas.

Audience calls
New installations often include loudspeakers in audience circulation areas such as foyers and bars so that—in addition to traditional bells—the stage manager can call the audience ('Ladies and Gentlemen, the curtain will rise in one minute' etc.).

Contact
Having stressed the need for good communication, it may seem perverse to go on to warn against too much of it. But there is a danger—particularly with the wearing of 'cans'—that the technical staff may get so involved in communicating that they lose contact with the show. Technicians, like actors, are not robots: without in any way departing from the details of the rehearsed framework, there is scope for subtle variations in timing. To be alive to this, the technician must be in contact (which is not quite the same as merely listening) with the show rather than cocooned in a communications network. One ear for the show, the other for the SM? This is not an easy point to make—it is all part of that indefinable 'what makes a live show live?'.

Organisation

To ensure the most efficient use of limited staging time, the sound department requires considerable advance planning. The amount of planning will vary with the type of production and the type of producing organisation. A company performing in its own theatre will probably have a comprehensive sound system, in which case planning will just be a case of preparing tapes and deciding if any microphones or loudspeakers need to be re-positioned. At the other extreme, a musical moving into a rented theatre may have to plan to hire and install every single item down to the last piece of cable.

Planning can be carried out under the headings already

discussed in this chapter.

Reinforcement planning requires the preparation of a detailed drawing showing microphone types and positions, speaker types and positions, and the assignment of mixer channels.

Effects planning starts from an acquisition list of effects. After editing, the tape should be played during final run-throughs in the rehearsal room to check on cue positions, length etc.

Communications planning requires decisions on the out-stations required for stage management cueing in performance together with an assessment of extra communication facilities required for the technical and dress rehearsal period.

9 Wardrobe

There was once a production of 'The Clandestine Marriage' where the director shouted, in the middle of the technical dress rehearsal, 'Stop, stop, hold it ... either we remake all the costumes or we widen all the doors.' This was of course an exaggeration and nothing drastic was done to either the doors or the costumes. The actors just had to make less than perfect exits and entrances for the next three months. It was sad that such a situation—doors narrowed for perspective, and skirt fullness increased for effect—should reach the final production weekend before discovery. More common is the impossible quick change which entails frantic alterations at the last minute. Yes, it's back to our old friend, *planning*!

Design

As with the other staging departments, our concern here is not with costume design but with wardrobe organisation: not the internal wardrobe organisation concerned with the cutting and making of costumes, but the organisation by which the wardrobe department integrates with everyone else. Nevertheless, design is never just a matter of visual aesthetics and there are a number of design practicalities to be raised and got out of the way at early production conferences.

In particular, before a costume design is approved by the director, there has to be consideration of whether the actor can work in it: singing and dancing can be difficult if not impossible in certain styles of costume and the designer will need to know if the actor is going to be called upon to do any complex movement.

Incidentally, the door problem mentioned above occurred in a production where there were separate designers for settings and costumes. In such circumstances the director and production manager need to keep an eye and an ear on the design partnership, ever ready to detect a lack of harmony not just over practical matters, but possibly over fundamentals like style and colour as well.

Wardrobe plot

The wardrobe plot is an actor-by-actor, scene-by-scene inventory of all the costumes in a production. It is a detailed breakdown which lists every separate item in each costume. It serves as a check list during budgeting, making, fittings, and when the clothes are packed and unpacked. Director and choreographer

A wardrobe plot.

```
'ROBINSON CRUSOE' THEATRE ROYAL/NEWCASTLE 1975/6


COSTUME PLOT


ACT ONE    PROLOGUE

BLACKBEARD                      Black Velvet Coat trimmed Gold Braid,
                                Black Shirt, Breeches, Belt, Boots,
                                Gloves, Black Hat with Skull and Cross-
                                bones, Red Cloak with Skull and Cross-
                                bones, Red Kerchief for head, Black
                                Kerchief for neck, Earrings, Chains.

FAIRY                           Green Lurex Leotard, Silk Chiffon Drapes
                                in shades of green, Tiara, Pink Tights,
                                Ballet Pointes or Green Court Shoes.


ACT ONE    SCENE 1              THE HARBOUR OF WHITLEY BAY

GIRL DANCERS                (1) Fishergirl Dresses in various colours
                                with White Petticoats attached, coloured
                                Kerchiefs for necks, White Briefs,
                                White Tights, Black Buckle Shoes.

                            (2) Red and White Striped Tee-Shirts, White
                                Trousers, Black Belts, Black Sailor Hats,
                                Tights and Shoes as above, Navy Blue Short
                                Jackets, Red Kerchiefs.

4  BOY SINGERS AND              Red and White Tee-Shirts, White Trousers,
1 EXTRA COSTUME                 Black Belts, Black Sailor Hats or Wool
                                Caps, White Socks, Black Buckle Shoes,
                                Navy Blue Jackets, Red Kerchiefs.

CRUSOE                          Navy Blue Jacket, Gold Briefs, Tan Tights,
                                Black Court Shoes, Lace Jabot and Cuffs.

POLLY                           Purple Velvet Bodice with White Organdie
                                Skirt decorated with Yellow Daisies,
                                White Petticoat attached, Yellow Briefs,
                                Tan Tights, Yellow Shoes, Yellow Hat,
                                Mauve Gloves.

MOTHER RILEY                    Own Costume.
```

have copies so that they know how individual chorus members will be dressed in any particular scene. This will affect grouping and choreographic patterns, so the director and choreographer need to know who is wearing what. The stage manager also has a copy and it can be useful if he provides labels for the first blocking rehearsals. Incidentally, this is a good moment for the SM to exercise his characteristic tact and develop his friendly relationship with the acting company—most people do not really like having labels stuck on them but with an explanation and a joke from the production and stage management teams all will be well and indeed, with the right approach, the chorus will be made to feel more like individuals.

Making

Whether costumes are made 'in house' in the theatre's own workrooms or whether they are made by outside contractors will depend on the type of production company mounting the show. Only companies with their own theatres or companies presenting regular long seasons in rented theatres are likely to have their own workrooms, and these workrooms are often concerned more with alterations to accommodate cast changes in revivals of old productions than in making for new productions. Even the biggest repertoire organisations are likely to have some of their costumes made 'out'—very often it is the highly specialised men's tailoring that is contracted out.

Hiring

For short runs, costumes may be rented under various arrangements between the extremes of everything being selected from stock, or everything made specially and then absorbed into the costumier's rental stock at the end of the run. There is a whole range of compromises between these extremes: decision will depend on budget and that elusive hunt for the most cost-effective way of spending the allocated money.

Rehearsal costumes

An actress in a full hooped skirt takes up more stage space than an actress in rehearsal jeans: there are restrictions on her movements and on her relations with other members of the cast. It is therefore useful—and is the practice in most opera companies particularly—to make petticoats of suitable fullness available in the rehearsal room. Hats can be tricky and it is useful for them to be available in advance of the final dress rehearsal period.

Fittings

Costume fittings are tricky to schedule. Costume making is invariably carried out against the clock and so once a costume has reached the point where a fitting is required, it is important to get actor, designer, cutter and costume together as soon as possible. In most productions there is a concentrated rehearsal period of three to five weeks with rehearsal sessions each and every day. Removing actors for fittings—usually at short notice—can play havoc with rehearsal schedules, particularly at the later stages of rehearsals when the play is being 'run' in longish sections.

A costume design by Theodor Pitsek (Czechoslovakia).

Scheduling the fittings is a little easier in repertoire theatres. The rehearsal period is spread over a longer period with shorter daily sessions and so it is a little easier to arrange fittings without removing actors from the rehearsal room. There can, however, be problems in the opera house where costumes sometimes have to be made to dubious measurements sent by post. The singer then may have to be rushed straight from airport to wardrobe.

An actor's first encounter with his unfinished costume can be a touch neurotic and this is understandable. If leads are being asked to wear designs in which they are thought to lack complete confidence, it is a good policy for the director to attend the first fitting to spread confidence.

Getting in

Production companies with their own theatres have all the necessary wardrobe equipment installed on a permanent basis and when such companies work in repertoire, there is an organisational framework to get the right costume to the right dressing room on the right day. A company going into a rented theatre, however, has to organise a 'get-in'. In addition to getting costumes to the theatre, it will be necessary to take in costume rails with dust sheets plus such standard items of wardrobe maintenance as washing machines, driers, irons, ironing boards, sewing machines, etc. It is sensible (but not always done) to check in advance that the electrical equipment has the right plugs.

Dress parades

On the day of the first dress rehearsal, or if possible on a day previous, it is usual and useful to hold a dress parade where all members of the cast put on each of their costumes in sequence and parade before director and designer together with the senior members of the team who have been responsible for cutting and making. Whenever possible the dress parade is held on stage so that the clothes can be seen at a distance and under stage lighting conditions. The dress parade is a chance to see the exact state of wardrobe preparation and detailed lists are prepared of missing items and alterations required. It is also a good moment to check such things as the matching of chorus groups; and anyone who thinks that they may have a movement or breathing problem will be quite vociferous about it at this time.

Dress rehearsals

At dress rehearsals, especially the first dress rehearsal, it is essential that a senior wardrobe person, preferrably *the* senior wardrobe person, sits with the production team in the

auditorium to take notes and to discuss with the director and designer any costume problems as they occur. If wardrobe preparations are behind, it is very tempting for all the wardrobe staff to be upstairs working on the uncompleted costumes. But this is a temptation to be resisted: if costumes are incomplete, it is particularly important for a senior person to be present to check that the missing items are in fact being made and to reassure everyone of that fact. With the possible exception of the very first rehearsal in dress, the dressers should always be present as for performance.

Quick changes

When simple quick changes are to be done in the wings, the dresser stands by with the change of clothes, helps the actor, then takes the discarded costume back to the dressing room. If the actor is going to drop any garments, the dresser should lay out a dust sheet on the stage floor to catch these. A few theatres have permanent quick change rooms adjacent to the stage: mostly, however, a complex quick change involves building a quick change room with scenery flats in a corner of the stage and installing chair, table, mirror, lights and probably a dress rail.

Dress rehearsal costume care

Dress rehearsals are the moment to instil costume discipline: no eating in costume, no sitting in the auditorium, etc. Technical stage work continues to be in progress between dress rehearsals: the stage floor may not therefore always be quite as clean as it will be at performances. To protect long dresses, it is useful to tack polythene over the lower few inches which will be in contact with the floor.

Wardrobe maintenance

Visually, there is nothing lets a show down quite so much as badly looked after costumes. The clean crisp look will help blind the audience to deficiencies in other areas, including many shortcomings in the actual design of the costumes. Even clothes that look dirty and crumpled must be cleaned and pressed for the dirt and crumple should arise from design not from lack of care. Wardrobe maintenance is like any other maintenance: routine planned overhauls in an attempt to avoid or at least minimise breakdowns. This means scheduling laundry, cleaning and pressing on a regular basis, coupled with actors' and dressers' co-operation in drawing the wardrobe staff's attention to the need for minor repairs as soon as that need arises.

Wigs

In opera and classical drama companies there is a separate wig department: otherwise wigs and hair pieces come under the umbrella of the wardrobe department. There is nothing quite so eye-catching as a badly dressed wig and so, unless the production uses enough wigs to justify a specialist on the staff, arrangements must be made for the wigs to be returned to a perruquier for regular dressing.

PART III
THE STAGING PROCESS

10 Staging the play

Now let us follow the staging of a play from the point where it gets possession of the stage until it opens to the public for performance. Let us assume that it is a play being produced for a 'run', rather than a play being slotted into a repertoire. Let us take as our starting point the state of preparation that the play should be in when it reaches its final run-through in the rehearsal room.

The *actors* will have developed to the pitch where they can go no further without the whole supporting environment of scenery, costumes, props, effects, music and lights. Indeed the acting intensity will now drop for a little time while they adjust to coping with the technicalities of the stage apparatus. Then the acting will start to rise again, now integrated with the staging until the production reaches the pitch where it can go no further without an audience. Building a company of actors to the right pitch at the right time, not too early and not too late, is a basic skill of the good director.

The *stage management* will have the prompt book absolutely up to date with all cues and warnings marked in as far as known. They will have double-checked on the state of preparations in the various departments and where they foresee snags they will have quietly prepared contingency plans, 'just in case'. Numbers of staff required for fit-up, rehearsals and performances will have been agreed with the departmental heads and the appropriate calls made. In the event of unforeseen circumstances playing havoc with the schedule, they will have checked the movements (in terms of telephone numbers) of all actors and staging personnel up to the time of their first 'call' on stage. They will have satisfied themselves that everyone has received and understood the schedule and they will have ensured that there is an ample stock of coffee, tea, milk and sugar to sustain themselves and their fellow workers in the hours ahead.

The *scenery* will be completely constructed and painted. It will be fitted with all necessary cleats, lines, pin hinges, and hanging irons, etc. If the workshop is big enough there will have been a trial set-up of sections, if not of the whole set. Edges of flattage or framed borders which show to the audience will not have been forgotten in the painting and where the lighting layout plan shows that light is likely to bleed through the canvas, the back of that canvas will have been painted opaque. Hanging wire, timber battening, hinge-pins, screws, screw-eyes, nuts, bolts and any other necessary ironmongery items will be ready—together with the tools to use them. All items of scenery will be marked in a way that corresponds to the stage and hanging plans. Scene change and fly plots will have been prepared and agreed with the stage management.

All *props* will have been made or selected with the smaller items being in use for the final days in the rehearsal room. Arrangements will have been made for a supply of expendable props such as food, drinks and smokes; and a sufficient number of disposable items like letters for tearing up and crocks for breaking will have been prepared for the period up to and a little beyond the opening night. All props will be check listed and plots prepared.

The *electrics* department will have prepared the lighting equipment required by the lighting design plan, additional equipment being hired where necessary. Cables will have the correct plugs and will be the appropriate lengths with some taped up into cable ropes when required for feeding bars. Accessories will be standing by and all colour filters will be cut to size. Non-production-lighting items like cue lights, working lights, motors, wardrobe equipment, etc., will be prepared. The lighting designer will have a cue synopsis agreed with director, designer, and stage manager; and the board operator will have a copy so that he can foresee tricky operational problems.

The *sound* tapes will be prepared and the principal effects

SUNDAY	
8.00	Get-in & fit-up
13.00 - 14.00	Lunch
14.00 - 18.00	Focus lights & plot cues. Dress set.
18.00 - 18.30	Break
18.45 - 23.00	Technical dress rehearsal

MONDAY	
9.00 - 13.00	Technical work on stage
12.30	Cast for notes in stalls bar
13.00 - 14.00	Lunch
14.15	Dress Rehearsal
19.40	Press photo on stage
20.00	First performance

Typical schedule for a simple play.

should have been tried out in the rehearsal room. Equipment will be ready, including kit for editing. The theatre's communication equipment will have been investigated and any necessary modifications such as extra outstations ordered. Rehearsal talk-back facilities for the production team's desk in the auditorium will be standing by.

The *wardrobe* will have had their final fittings and the clothes will be ready to wear. The theatre's wardrobe maintenance equipment will have been appraised and any necessary additions ordered.

Scheduling

Unless the play is particularly complicated or is being produced in particularly luxurious circumstances, the maximum time

SUNDAY

01.00	Get-in and commence fit-up (stage & electrics)
10.00	Commence focussing (1 flyman standing-by). Stage continue building trucks in dock
12.00 - 13.00	Stage lunch break
13.00 - 14.00	Electrics lunch break
14.00	Carry on focussing
15.00 approx	Commence plotting
18.00 - 19.00	Stage & electrics break Director set sound levels
19.15 - 23.00	Act I stopping dress, no make-up
23.00	Continue lighting as necessary

MONDAY

08.00 - 12.00	Technical work on stage
12.00 - 13.00	Staff lunch
12.00	Cast photo-call
13.30	Act II stopping dress (N.B. Some show staff not available)
18.30 - 19.30	Break
20.00	Full Dress Rehearsal
23.00	Stage free for painters

TUESDAY

09.00 - 13.00	Technical work on stage
12.00	Company for notes in the stalls (Stage available from 1 pm)
13.00 - 14.00	Staff break
14.15	Dress rehearsal. No make-up (N.B. Full show staff not available)
20.00	First performance

Typical schedule for a more complex play.

likely to be available will be from after the get-out of the previous show on Saturday night/Sunday morning until curtain up on Tuesday. This means about 65 hours, or for a Monday opening about 40 hours. There is a temptation to feel that because all these hours exist, they should be worked. But night work leads to decreasing efficiency on the following day and certainly no one should ever be asked (or allowed) to work two consecutive nights while continuing by day. The two schedules shown here illustrate the sort of proportioning of time that has been found practical for simple and not-quite-so-simple plays.

Unloading

An efficient get-in begins with planned unloading. The basic aim is to avoid double-handling wherever possible: as each item is removed from the van it must be carried directly to a position on the stage as close as possible to where it will be required. Wardrobe baskets and dress rails are, naturally, taken straight to the wardrobe and if the stage is particularly small or the play particularly large, it may be desirable to 'lay-off' certain bulky items which are not required until a late point in the fit-up—let's hope that there is a roomy scene dock or that there is an alleyway and the sun is shining. Let's hope that the sun is shining anyway, for very few get-ins are under cover. If there is an apron stage, it may prove a useful dumping ground for lighting equipment and/or bulky furniture. In modern theatres there is often a motorised orchestra pit which doubles as an apron and it is worthwhile bringing it up to stage level for the period of the fit-up. Flats which have been stowed on their sides in the van should be raised upright as they are brought in and should be stacked against the wall so that the first items required are not buried at the bottom of the pack. To make all this happen, the play's master carpenter, who is going to be in charge of the fit-up, should stand on stage and assign a position to every item as it is carried in.

Hanging

Occasionally, very occasionally, the lighting equipment is got-in and rigged before the scenic fit-up starts, but normally the lighting rigging and scenic fit-up are carried out simultaneously. This calls for careful integration. It is logical for both departments to start by hanging all their flown stuff and if the stage staff start upstage and the electrics downstage, this usually works. Once the lighting bars are flown, the electrics can move to the side of the stage to prepare booms, etc., and into the auditorium to work on FOH.

Setting line

Scenery is positioned on the stage with reference to the centre line and the setting line. The centre line is (or should be) obvious but do not assume that it coincides with the middle of the centre aisle in the auditorium: old theatre architecture is often considerably off-centre. The centre line should be permanently marked at the front of the stage, as well as on the stage side of the fire-curtain and on every bar of the flying system. The setting line runs parallel to the front of the stage and its position will have been decided on the ground plans in advance. After it has been struck (usually with a chalked line), the company stage manager and lighting designer should confer with the master carpenter to check that there will be no problems arising from setting furniture upstage of the house curtain or in lighting from the theatre's fixed positions. These matters will (or should) have been considered in the early planning discussions but there are facts of theatre architecture that do not show up clearly on theatre plans and sections even when these are accurate and up-to-date. The actors and their director always wish to set as far downstage as possible and this makes sense—always providing that getting near the audience does not introduce horrendous problems which will more than offset the gain in audience contact. Compromise as always is the order of the day: but it must be stressed that the setting line decision is a vitally important one.

The flyman's view of a play with a ceiling.

Fitting up

After everything has been hung and flown clear of the stage, the floor is laid. This may be a simple painted stage cloth, but in the design of today's plays it is likely to be a built structure, almost certainly raked and probably shaped to define an acting 'island' area. The *standing* parts of the set are built next: that is, any pieces which are permanent to the extent of not being moved during performance. The whole set may be standing or just parts of it. The changeable pieces are prepared in the wings and each scene may now be *set and marked* as the jargon has it: meaning each scene set up and the positions of scenery and furniture marked on the floor. To save time, unless particular difficulties are anticipated, setting and marking can be left until each scene is set-up during the lighting rehearsal—there is then usually quite a lot of time available to consider problems while the lighting cues are plotted. Moreover all the production team are likely to be present to decide on any compromise that may be required. Temporary marks are usually made with adhesive tape and more permanent ones with paint. Colour coding can be used to differentiate between scenes. Marks must be as small and as few as is practicable otherwise they become not only visible to the audience but confusing to the staff.

Electrics rigging

The bars are by far the quickest part of the electrics rigging operation, but before any bar is flown above stage level it is wise to check it by *flashing out*. Each of the plug tops at the end of the cable-rope or multicore cable feeding the bar is made live in turn, usually by utilising a convenient independent power socket on the side of the stage. As each lamp is checked and proved to be working, its circuit number should be chalked on the plug top. While this is happening, another electrician should check that all gobos, irises, etc., are fitted, that all colours are in, that all profile shutters are fully out, that all barndoors are open, that all safety chains are secure and that all hanging nuts are tight. Once flown, the bar is plugged to the dimmer control system and this is usually through a permanent socket box on the fly floor. Booms and ladders take more time to rig as they involve spotting special lines from the grid unless (and this rarely happens) the fly rail is in precisely the correct position. Booms should be lifted on to a couple of stage weights while their supporting lines are tied-off: this ensures that the line is taut when the base is screwed into the stage floor. In most theatres, with the exception of some commercial houses in London and New York, most of the FOH spotlights in the auditorium will be permanent and may need little or no augmentation with extra instruments. They will, however, need colouring and this is an activity that can be usefully slotted in while the stage is occupied by scenery construction. The practice of colouring each lantern as it is focused is very wasteful in terms of time.

Deading

The word *dead* has various and confusing meanings. We are here talking about deciding the heights of flown pieces, both scenic and electric. Chapter 5 discussed top and bottom flying deads and also the term *deadline* used to describe a suspension line which is permanently fixed rather than workable from the flys. *Dead it* with reference to a piece of scenery means get rid of it—so *dead scenery* is scenery that has been built for the production but discarded. Keeping scenery *live* on the other hand usually means that items coming off in a scene change are going to repeat in a later scene and should not be buried at the bottom of the pack. All just a touch confusing!

The deading of the lighting bars and masking borders must be finalised before any of the lighting equipment is focused. In theory the deads (or to use an American term now becoming more commonly used in Britain, the *trims*) will have been decided by a study of the section drawings at the planning stage and will be marked on the drawings. In practice, inspired guesswork is often substituted for accurate calculation and the quality of the inspiration varies. Either way a little flexibility is possible until focusing is commenced. After this point second thoughts can be rather expensive. The deading is best done by the master carpenter, advised by a committee of scene designer, lighting designer and stage manager. The designer watches from the auditorium while the master carpenter instructs his fly staff from the front row of seating. The lighting designer is mainly interested in checking from the stage that his lights will be able to reach their intended targets, while the stage manager goes between stage and auditorium, keeping a particular eye on sightlines from the back of the gallery. The checklist of points to be watched (and if necessary compromised between) is design, lighting, masking and sightline. The same process has to be carried out for the side masking and in both cases it may be necessary to accept inferior masking from front rows and inferior sightline from high back rows because making things perfect for the few might spoil them for the many.

Focusing

When rigging of the lighting has been completed, the lighting designer should have a quick flash-through of all circuits to check the rig against the plan. Calling the circuit numbers one by one (either in geographical or, probably better, in numerical sequence) ensures that everything is working and that the channel numbers on the control correspond to those on the plan. Wrongly numbered plans are a standard source of time-wasting confusion during the focusing and plotting of lighting: this is the point in the schedule to eliminate that possibility. A flash-through at this point will also give some indication of whether a lantern is likely to be able to do the job assigned to it. For one reason or another, foreseeable or unforeseeable, the light may not be able to hit the desired part of the stage. If this is recognised now, the lighting designer may be able to swop functions between lanterns without altering the rig or possibly by swopping colour filters only.

And so, on to the laborious job of setting each lantern by adjusting its direction and its beam size, shape and quality. Access is the main problem and more time is spent in moving and climbing ladders than on actually adjusting lanterns. In modern theatres, most FOH spotlights are accessible from cat-walks; older theatres built before the era of modern lighting require the electrician to be something of a gymnast. On stage it is a matter of ladders and the traditional 'A' ladders have been superseded by a proprietary form of alloy vertical ladder on an adjustable wheeled base, called a *tallescope*, which has become standard in British theatres and has simplified the ladderwork of all departments. (Indeed, sharing the tallescope is a vital part of interdepartmental co-ordination, as most playhouses are so small that two tallescopes cause traffic congestion.) To focus lights there must be one electrician up the ladder and one on the control board. There is a very positive saving of expensive time if two people are assigned to pushing the tallescope around. The lighting designer can do this, but between lamps he should be looking at his plan rather than moving ladders. Focusing is normally done one lamp at a time unless the join between two lamps is being checked. When the new channel number is called, this should be brought on before the previous one is turned off. This saves time and promotes safety by preventing the stage from going to complete blackout. Ideally, the only light on stage during focusing will be from the light currently being worked on, but in reality props and stage are likely to be still working as well and they will require some working light although this must of necessity be limited in its brightness and in the area covered. This is another of these areas of co-ordination and one where split mealtimes and even split coffee breaks can allow a particular department to have sole occupancy of the stage for a critical task. If the design uses several complete settings, then all these will be required in turn for focusing. In more skeletal scenic styles, most of the lights will be focused to the basic set with the various scenic elements being flown in or carried on for the angling of appropriate lanterns. If there are many flying pieces, a flyman should stand-by throughout; and a member of the stage management team should always be on call to advise on furniture and actor positions.

Plotting the lighting

After the focusing comes the actual 'lighting'—the composition of the lighting pictures as a series of cues for the control board. The director and designer sit with the lighting designer at the production desk in the auditorium and they should be joined by the member of the stage management team (probably the DSM) who is going to give the cues as part of his running of the play from the prompt corner. At least one ASM is available to 'walk', that is to take up various actor positions on stage, and the

Access by tallescope.

company stage manager stands by to organise scene changes and to discuss with the team the various technical matters that always crop up at this time. In addition to his plan, the lighting designer has his cue synopsis which has been agreed previously with the director and designer; and the DSM has used his copy of the synopsis to pencil the cues into the prompt book. The SM should have a copy to keep him in the picture and to enable him to check progress and warn the crew when to stand by for changes. The board operator's copy will be specially marked with the time between cues as a guide to the time available for resetting the control panels.

Scenes are set up exactly and completely, including all furniture and dressings. This will probably be the first time that the director has seen the complete settings on stage and he will probably want to experiment with furniture positions while the lighting designer builds the basic lighting picture. This is also the moment to list missing items and jobs to be done. Under lighting, some problems disappear but fresh ones are discovered. Some darkening or texturing of the painting may be necessary in certain areas to take down the harshness from actor lights which unavoidably hit the scenery.

When the lighting designer thinks that he is near to achieving the state of a particular cue, he will seek the opinion of the designer and director who will move the ASM(s) about the stage to check actor light in key positions. The lighting designer will have one eye on his watch and as problems arise he must decide whether there is time to tackle them now or whether to suggest that they be noted for future action.

When a cue is agreed, the board is asked to plot: the operator must not be hustled but given enough time to plot the levels accurately. This can take some time, particularly on the older types of system, but the wait provides a useful opportunity for the team to discuss the next cue. The cue synopsis is only a guide and need not be adhered to exactly if the business of lighting stimulates some good alternative (and practical) ideas. As soon as plotted, it's on with the next cue. There is seldom time with older equipment to 'see the effect of the cue change and check its timing'; this is a bonus that comes with the latest memory controls. Otherwise it is better to move on and leave the finer details of timing to the technical dress rehearsals—although, of course, basic timings will have been decided, included in the cue synopsis, and possibly amended while lighting.

Sound effect levels

As the lighting proceeds, the time for the first rehearsal is fast approaching. Somehow the director has to find time to set sound levels and this probably involves having sandwiches brought to the theatre while everyone else goes out for a more relaxed meal. This is the moment to check the directional placing of the effects loudspeakers and to decide a level for each sound cue.

Actors on stage

Actors need time to familiarise themselves with the set. The geography of some designs can be quite complex and even the simplest box setting of a drawing room can spring a few surprises. No matter how well a rehearsal room has been marked out certain moves, particularly entrances and exits, can only be finally timed in the complete set. Familiarisation may just be individual actors informally trying out their moves or a more formal rehearsal to modify some bit of business that the director, having seen the set, has realised will not quite work. This familiarisation is conveniently carried out in the gap between the end of the lighting rehearsal and the beginning of the technical dress since the staff need time at this point to take a break before they get set-up for the beginning of the play.

Dress parade

For a small cast play, a formal dress parade is unlikely to be required. The costume designer will be able to see all the cast individually in the dressing rooms and the director will look them over as they come on stage for rehearsal. For plays with lots of supporting actors, a dress parade becomes another of the events to be squeezed in somewhere—probably just prior to the technical dress. The state of the costumes at the final fittings will have given some indication of how long the dress parade is likely to take and if the stage schedule is tight, then the event can be diverted to somewhere like the stalls bar.

Technical rehearsal

There is normally little point in running through a play's technical cues without the cast. If all members of all departments—stage, flys, props, electrics and sound—have properly plotted cue sheets, it is time to try to put it all together with the actors. If time permits, there may be a case for rehearsing scene changes but the crew (with the possible exception of showmen) will have done the changes at least once during the lighting, and possibly twice if there was a separate setting and marking session. It is probably better, therefore, to move on to a stopping dress rehearsal and possibly hold a separate technical later to polish the trickier moments.

Technical dress rehearsal

This is sometimes called a stopping rehearsal or a stagger-through. The object is to solve every problem as it arises, stopping wherever necessary. The actors give restrained performances, concentrating on moves and 'business' rather than projecting character. This rehearsal is a critical one and it is important to avoid panic. The actors are anxious and the staff are tired. The word 'impossible' may be heard from time to time and it is very important for members of the production team to be able to differentiate between the definitely impossible and the merely difficult. Many good effects have been lost at this point by premature cuts made in panic. On the other hand, when something definitely does not work an alternative must be found—preferably now but certainly before the next rehearsal. How does one decide on difficult versus impossible? Well, remember that although the actors have been at it for weeks, the staff have only just started in the last couple of days or even hours to come to grips with an unfamiliar play and its unfamiliar cue sheets. With a bit of positive thinking one realises how well everyone is doing rather than how badly: how much they are getting right rather than how much they are getting wrong. The key persons in this stagger-through rehearsal process are the director and stage manager. They must be able to assess the weight that various members of their teams give to words like yes, no, difficult, easy, impossible, try and tomorrow. The role of the stage manager has been discussed in Chapter 4 and it must be repeated here that whereas the director may shout 'stop!', the SM must be the one to tell the actors when to start again and where to start from. And he will only do this after he has ascertained that everyone is ready and has set back to the appropriate cue state.

The problem in a stopping rehearsal is to keep some sort of momentum going despite the breaks—success is urging everyone on without alienating them. A knife-edge process! This rehearsal should include the procedure for fading houselights and curtain-up, etc., otherwise the next rehearsal will get off to a bad start. Topping and tailing (cutting dialogue between technical cues) should be avoided unless time shortage makes it absolutely essential. Anyway, unless it is a very simple play, topping and tailing often wastes as much time as it saves due to the time necessary to tell everyone where the restart is and for them to get set up. And the very dialogue section that is cut may include the very point where an actor has a door problem.

There should be no need for a note session after the technical dress. Representatives of all departments will have been watching with the director, discussing and noting problems as they occur. Everyone will have amended their plots and cue sheets and the net result will be that every actor and every technician is exhausted but knows what is supposed to happen.

Dress rehearsals

From this point onwards, the aim is to run without stopping: notes are made of any problems that arise or alterations that are required. Inevitably the rehearsal may come to a grinding halt from time to time, particularly if there are tricky scene changes. For the sake of the actor's concentration, the length of any such stops should be kept to a minimum. Better to pick up the threads as soon as possible, then have an inquest afterwards. Many of the notes arising from the dress rehearsal can be dealt with by discussion but some scenic, prop and lighting matters require exclusive or shared use of the stage. Priorities must be established so that stage time before the next dress rehearsal can be allocated: this will probably include a session for the actors. As the dress rehearsals progress, the number of notes taken is unlikely to get fewer, but they should gradually begin to be about increasingly subtle matters, particularly timing. The point to get worried is when the same notes have to be made at two rehearsals.

Press and photo calls

A special call for posed production photographs is now largely a thing of the past. Publicity photographs are taken as action shots during the course of dress rehearsals. The actors should be warned that it is happening and the photographer should be advised about unfinished scenery or costumes. A *press call* has to be slotted into the dress rehearsal schedule: a convenient time for both actors and press is a pre-lunch drinks reception for interviews and photographs. Some of the cast, particularly the young ladies, may be in costume. No matter how badly things are going on stage, a press call must be considered as an inviolate arrangement.

Final dress rehearsal

Plays often have only two dress rehearsals: a technical dress and a final. If there is any degree of technical complication in the show it is unfair to have less than three—unfair to the audience as well as author, actors and technicians. Normally the final dress is carried through absolutely as performance with the actors trying to cover up mistakes. If the play is a comedy it may be advisable to have a small invited audience to help the actors begin to time the laughs. The final dress rehearsal may have to be during the afternoon of the first performance and there may be difficulty in having a full staff if part-time showmen are being used. However, this is not too disastrous if the scene changes have already been proved to be possible. This final rehearsal belongs to the actors. The production team should be able to take a back seat: if they have done their job properly, it will be virtually over.

Previews and first performance

A production may play to an audience before its official opening or *first night* when the press are invited. The preview performances prior to this are not for experiment but to allow the production to mature with the help of audience response. During this period, the actors, and often the design team, need the protection of the director from the well-meaning advice offered by a brigade of assorted friends, relatives and agents' wives. A word from the wrong person in the right ear has been known to cause a re-write of torpedo effect.

It should almost have to go without saying that the production team never, but never, interfere with the running of any performance. No matter what happens, their role is to grit their teeth and make their notes. The stage manager is in total charge once the half-hour has been called.

11 Staging the musical

The difference between a musical and a play is not so much the music but the size. There are, of course, exceptions but even a small standing-set musical play like 'The Fantasticks' uses a company of 15 actors and musicians, a number that is relatively large by the standard of most contemporary plays. There is more to integrate in a musical. There are various groups (principals, chorus and orchestra) indulging in various activities (speaking, singing and dancing) and these group activities have to be rehearsed in every combination. The solitary author becomes a team of writers with separate responsibilities for book, lyrics and music; while the director becomes the chairman of a directing team that includes the choreographer and musical director.

Prior to get-in

The technical departments have to prepare more of most things: more scenery, more lights, more costumes and more sound. The props department are likely to have less fiddly set dressings but more big props, and while there may be fewer different kinds of hand props, some may be required in quantities of around forty.

The stage management team have a tough job arranging rehearsals. Several adjacent rehearsal rooms are required with intricate rehearsal schedules to shuffle actors to the correct dialogue, musical or choreographic session. In each type of session actors may work singly, in assorted pairs, trios or ensembles as everything is gradually brought together. Scheduling rehearsal pianists can be one of the trickier aspects of this operation. It is not possible to bring a musical into quite as finalised a rehearsal room state as can be done with a play. A final run-through will show an integration of the acting, singing and dancing in each individual scene but the links between the scenes are likely to be sketchy. In a modern musical particularly, the stage action is continuous and is integrated choreographically and musically with the changing scenery.

During the final days in the rehearsal room, the orchestra may have started to rehearse on their own and may have been joined by actors for musical rehearsal but it is not until the show goes on to the stage with the orchestra in the pit that the action can be integrated with the orchestrations.

Scheduling

It will be appreciated from all this that a musical requires more time between get-in and opening than does a straight play. More time to fit up and more time to rehearse. It is difficult to avoid a lot of overnight work and in the big commercial musicals a combination of various methods is used to make 24-hour progress without causing excessive fatigue.

For a big fit-up in London, extra staff are borrowed from other theatres and it should be possible to work out some sort of shift system so that everyone gets at least minimum sleep without progress being halted. After the basic initial fit-up is completed, day and night work can be split between departments; or, probably more productive, the stage can be handed over to the actors for familiarisation rehearsal by day while technical work continues by night. Painters have a lot of touching up to do and painting of the floor is a job usually done on site rather than in the studio: this is best done by leaving the painters on their own in the theatre overnight with lots of light. And there never was a musical whose rehearsals failed to throw up some problems requiring technical alterations of one kind or another.

It has to be a very simple musical to be able to get in on Sunday and open on Tuesday. It can be done and will continue to be done but a successful opening performance under these circumstances relies on an exceptionally experienced technical staff as well as on planning—plus lots of luck and a good measure of adrenalin to produce the magic that pulls a show through by substituting attack for polish.

Getting in and fitting up

There are always exceptions, but generally a musical has more scenery than a play: more volume, more complexity and more changes. Older musicals alternated big full stage scenes with painted front cloths which gave a large staff time to do complete scene changes and a large chorus time to do complete costume changes. More recent musicals aim for continuity by incorporating visible scene changes into the action. They use a permanent decorative surround which gives a stylistic unity to scenic elements dropped in from the flys or brought on from the sides using trucks (or, occasionally, revolves).

To move the trucks magically without visible manual assistance but with precision, a big long run musical is set on a specially designed false stage floor. This has track grooves cut into it to guide the trucks which are moved by steel wire cables

Detailed schedule for the gct-in of 'Man of La Mancha'. The full schedule, drawn up by Ian Albery as Production Manager, included the countdown (re-routing of services, etc.) prior to the conclusion of the previous show and consequent removal of the stage flooring, so that the setting could be built up from the basement floor. After the run of 'Man of La Mancha', the Piccadilly Theatre was equipped with a modular removable stage floor.

in the couple of inches of void space between the real stage and the false stage. The trucks are usually moved by hand operated winches although motors can and have been used. Any such false floor has to be laid as the first operation of the fit-up: this means that it has to be the first item to be unloaded and got in to the theatre. If dock space is tight, it may be necessary to lay the floor before unloading anything else. Next step, as in a play, is the hanging, although this is likely to be much more complex with lots of french flats to be built. The number of hangings in a musical is often greater than the number of counterweight lines available and extra lines, sometimes temporary counterweights but usually hemp, are installed. The hangings are then so tightly packed that brail lines may have to be run across from one fly gallery to the other to make space for a flown piece to move on cue by easing adjacent non-moving pieces upstage or downstage out of the way. Hanging must be completed before the masking

STAGE	ELECTRICS
WEDNESDAY APRIL 3rd **8.00 a.m.** Fit-up rear platform bridge (Hall's) **9.00 a.m.** Hetherington's start laying felt and rubber flooring and making good fibre-glass joints (work all night, if necessary, to complete by Thursday lunch-time) Stage staff break when fit-up completed, and after checking that Hall's and Hetherington's require no assistance. **2.00 p.m.** Scenic artists (G. Guy) start painting main set (work all night)	Remove dust-sheets from spot bars. Set-up and check intercom systems, cue lights, blue lights, etc, and sound effects system. Complete preparations for focussing. Provide good work-light overnight for scenic artists.
THURSDAY APRIL 4th **9.00 a.m.** Hall's & Harry Pegg) + 6 men Harry Robinson) Lower cyc and cut hole, and lower quatrefoil frame, as necessary, to allow lifting bridge to hinge on to fixed platform bridge. Test lifting bridge mechanically. **3.00 p.m.** NB: At least one skilled flyman should be on duty on counter-weight system while focussing in progress from cradles with a second responsible person at stage level.	Test lifting bridge electrically. Focussing until last transport
FRIDAY 5th APRIL **9.00 a.m.** Set up props etc (Stage Management) Fit new orchestra posts & chains (Hall's) **7.30 p.m.** ARTISTS REHEARSE ON STAGE	Continue focussing until finished. WORKING LIGHT ONLY
SATURDAY 6th APRIL **9.00 a.m.** **10.00 a.m.**	Prepare for lighting Plot lighting through until last transport
SUNDAY 7th APRIL ARTISTS REHEARSE ON STAGE ALL DAY	WORKING LIGHT ONLY
MONDAY 8th APRIL **9.00 a.m.** Prepare for Technical Rehearsal **7.00 p.m.** FIRST TECHNICAL REHEARSAL WITH LIGHTING (TO FINISH BEFORE LAST TRANSPORT, EVEN IF ONLY PARTIALLY COMPLETED)	Complete plotting
TUESDAY 9th APRIL **Morning:** Technical work on stage Stretch cyc properly and lay floor panels. **Afternoon:** ARTISTS REHEARSE ON STAGE **6.00 p.m.** TECHNICAL REHEARSAL (EITHER PICK UP FROM WHERE STOPPED PREVIOUS NIGHT, OR BEGIN AGAIN FROM TOP)	Technical work on stage WORKING LIGHT ONLY
WEDNESDAY 10th APRIL **Morning:** Technical work on stage **Afternoon:** ARTISTS REHEARSE ON STAGE **6.00 p.m.** : FIRST DRESS REHEARSAL (FULL – EX ORCHESTRA?)	Technical work WORKING LIGHT ONLY

surround is built because the full clear stage area is required for laying down and battening out the flown flats. The decorative masking usually consists of a series of *portals*, each formed from a pair of wing flats joined by a framed border. The downstage portal is called the false proscenium, shortened to *false pros*.

Basically the fit-up processes outlined for plays in the last chapter are applicable to musicals. The main differences are naturally scale and time, and the effect of this on inter-departmental co-ordination has been discussed under schedul-ing. Some other points of difference to be considered are ...

Lighting

There is a lot of lighting to focus: much of it is general, some is specific to particular scenes. The best procedure is probably to move through the rig in sequence, focusing as much as possible on a stage empty except for permanent masking but with a flyman standing by to drop in flown pieces as required. Spotlights which can only be focused to a built set should be passed over or perhaps just roughly set. After the general focusing session has been completed, scenes which have several special spotlights can be built for focusing. If a scene is complicated to build and/or only has one or two specials, it may be more economic to leave the focusing of these until the scene is built during the lighting plotting session. Side lighting (booms and ladders) tends to be general as does much of the FOH: so it is sensible to start with one of these, remembering that it is easier to shout instructions to the FOH when the theatre is quiet, perhaps during a split meal break. The lighting rehearsal, in addition to plotting light cues, is the time to clarify the co-ordination of scenery and lighting movements in the scene changes. Even after detailed planning, the most effective way of doing such moves often does not become obvious until this point (but planning is still required: it is easier to alter a plan than to have no plan at all).

Backstage at a musical (Her Majesty's Theatre, London)

Limes

Musicals usually have follow spots: at least two, often three and occasionally more. Both the follow spot and its operator are frequently referred to as *limes* although it is a long time since a piece of lime made incandescent in a gas jet was the light source. Most follow spots now use discharge lamps but several theatres still have older carbon arc types which are hot and smelly, although most of them are mechanically superior to the newer units. One operational snag of arcs is that the carbons require renewal during each act and convenient moments have to be plotted: often during a solo number when only one lime is required. Planned carbon changing, not surprisingly, is thrown by a stopping rehearsal. Ideally the lime operators should watch a run-through, preferably with the lighting designer, to get an overall familiarity with the show. Alternatively, the principals should be brought in front of the curtain to be introduced to the limes before the first technical dress rehearsal.

Technical rehearsals

Musicals inevitably involve the use of part-time staff, therefore full scale technical and dress rehearsing is only practicable in the evening. Day rehearsals can solve the technical problems of working in individual scenes: entrances, exits, use of levels, spacing of choreography, etc. There are a lot of matters that can be cleaned up by actors, choreographer and director in each set. The lighting designer can start to check the balance of some of his cues against the actor positions and the sound man can start to check on his microphone pick-up problems, although it will be too early to start sound balancing as not only will there be no orchestra but the actors will not be singing out.

If problems within scenes are worked on in this way, the

evening technical stagger-throughs can be devoted to the problems which concern everyone: the links to get out of one scene and into the next. To do the job properly on a big show needs two evenings: Act I tonight and Act II tomorrow. This allows technical problems to be sorted out before the orchestra joins to add a whole new series of musical problems.

Musical rehearsals

The first *band calls* held in a rehearsal room, often the theatre bar, are to sort out the notes. Singers join later band calls as a check on the correctness of the accompaniments and to familiarise themselves with the orchestrations. But it is only once the orchestra is in the pit that balance between voice and instruments can be worked out, including fold-back levels for the singers to hear not just the orchestra but their own voices. Also it is only at this point that choreographer and conductor can finalise the dance tempi, and the dancers be given a chance to synchronise with the totally different sound of the orchestra compared with a rehearsal piano. Most of this can be done without scenery: or essential bits such as levels built in skeleton form only. During such a rehearsal, the sound plot begins to take shape and the sound mixer operator should be given some idea of the extent to which individual singers are saving their voices rather than singing out.

Dress rehearsals

Orchestral time is very expensive and orchestral overtime is paid for in sacks of gold. It makes sense, therefore, to have done two things thoroughly before a full dress rehearsal: first, to have rehearsed the whole show technically with piano and, secondly, to have rehearsed individual scenes on stage with orchestra. To rush into full orchestral dress rehearsal without this groundwork can only result in expensive, depressing chaos. But with the suggested preparation, the first dress rehearsal should hold together with scene changes as the only really tricky moments. That there may be too much or too little scene change music may not be discovered until this point because a rehearsal pianist can 'vamp till ready' more easily than can a full orchestra. To get through a full dress rehearsal evening without the show falling apart is a splendid morale boost to everyone—but especially to the actors who can now concentrate on matters like characterisation and pace rather than the struggle to master technicalities, which has been their concern since leaving the rehearsal room.

Musical hysteria

It would be unrealistic to fail to mention at this point that the big musicals are very rarely staged in an atmosphere of calm. They stretch available resources and they stretch people, requiring detailed co-ordination between a bunch of individualists. And they represent a big financial investment. Everyone has a cure for the show's problems, whether they be real or imaginary, and often the best bits of the show are the ones that get cut. It is a rare commercial musical that reaches curtain up on the opening night without someone walking out or getting fired. There is no magical recipe for avoiding the contagious panic that causes all this —but good planning and communications help to create a sense of purpose and a feeling that progress is being made. And these are major requirements for creating a happy company.

12 Staging opera

Our discussion of plays and musicals has assumed that they were being staged for a 'run'—that they had sole occupancy of the stage for the period covering their staging rehearsals and performances, that is, sole occupancy from get-in to get-out. Most plays and musicals, at least in Anglo-American theatre practice, are mounted in this way but in turning our attention to *opera* we are looking at a stage form which is almost always played in *repertoire*, or that variation of repertoire known as *stagione* and already discussed in Chapter 2. Opera is performed in repertoire mainly to conserve the singers' voices: the strain of sustaining a big role every night will wreck a voice, particularly in its formative years. Also a repertoire programme suits the opera audience who like to see favourite established operas on a regular repeating basis, whereas most playgoers thrive on a diet of new drama. (Again we are speaking mainly of Anglo-American theatre; things are rather different in Central Europe where drama is also played largely in repertoire and with a strong classical bias.)

Some of the problems discussed in this chapter are special to opera but many of them are general repertoire problems arising out of the special circumstances of performing and rehearsing several shows concurrently, whether they be operatic, balletic or dramatic.

Opera companies

There are two kinds of opera companies: *permanent* and *ad hoc*. The permanent companies perform in their own theatres with full-time orchestra, chorus, and technicians. They have a nucleus of singers under annual contract but rely heavily for leads upon a pool of freelance singers—national or international depending on the status of the company. Ad hoc companies are formed for short seasons or for special performances at festivals. Even if an ad hoc company is only performing one opera, it generally has to be organised on repertoire lines as the stage is likely to be used by other performances during the season.

Rehearsals

Opera rehearsals are two-part: musical and production. Before the first production rehearsal, the singers study their roles individually with a repetiteur (a pianist-coach, probably with conducting ambitions). There are also ensemble musical rehearsals and so every member of the cast comes to the first production rehearsal knowing their part. As a result, production rehearsals can be more concentrated. Fewer sessions are required than with other forms of theatre but because the singers are performing during the evenings—in the same opera house or elsewhere—the rehearsals tend to be spread over a longer period. This spreading of rehearsals applies to the technical and dress rehearsals as well as to the earlier rehearsal room sessions. Because of daily performances, the pattern of use of the stage tends to be morning rehearsals, afternoon preparations for performance, then evening performance. For the preparation of a particularly heavy rehearsal or performance, overnight working can be added. Most round-the-year opera houses have two technical crews working a shift system, sometimes overlapping at the heaviest part of the day, the afternoon changeover from rehearsal to performance. Since the stage is only available for rehearsals in the mornings, the staging period is spread over something like a fortnight. There are advantages in that some of the pressure is removed and time is available between rehearsals for a re-think of any problems that have appeared. On the other hand, big disadvantages stem from the requirement that the whole technology of the production must be geared to quick setting and striking on a twice daily basis.

Schedules

There is an extra element in opera scheduling, always referred to as 'NA's', meaning non-availabilities. Singers may not be able to rehearse on certain days because they are resting before a particularly strenuous evening performance. Or freelances may be performing or rehearsing elsewhere. Small part singers may be rehearsing for two productions at the same time: it is common for an opera house to have one production in dress rehearsal while the next is in the rehearsal room. And the chorus may be NA on a particular day to avoid incurring overtime payments. Wherever possible NAs are agreed at the time of signing contracts, but to foster good relations with popular singers, managements often grant extra NAs at short notice. It is therefore not unknown for important rehearsals to include understudies, or 'covers' as they are more generally known in the opera world.

Long term schedules block out the allocation of stage, pit and the various rehearsal rooms on a sessional basis; and to permit

planning of alterations, this schedule should contain an NA column. Additionally, a detailed schedule is published daily giving a breakdown of each rehearsal and performance into the times at which various performers and personnel are called.

The London Opera Centre: a large cinema converted for use as an opera rehearsal room.

Rehearsal rooms

Opera production rehearsal rooms have to be large—at least as large as the stage's full acting area—because of the large numbers in the cast, the large gestures that they make, and the large volume of sound that they produce. There is also a large production team to be accommodated: director, conductor, choreographer, chorus master, coaches and stage management. And they all have assistants. Because of the nature of operatic scenery and the intensive rehearsal programme, it is desirable that at least the various scenic levels be provided for rehearsals. Special rehearsal rooms are often built to make this possible: at Glyndebourne, for example, there is a rehearsal stage on the same level as the main stage and trucked scenery can be moved from stage to rehearsal stage during the singers' lunch break.

Fitting up

A new production generally gets on to the stage about ten or more days before the first performance. The ideal day is a

production Sunday or whatever day of the week is the particular opera house's closed day (closure on both Sunday and Monday simplifies the whole operation). As the scenery is made for rapid daily setting and striking, it should go up relatively easily, even at first attempt. Opera stage facilities vary a great deal. Some have enough space adjacent to the stage to permit all trucks to be kept built for the current repertoire, others have to break down the trucks daily and some even have to get operas out daily for transport to distant storage. The big German-inspired stages of Central Europe have full side and rear stages which can be driven on to the main acting area, complete with full sets. These may be used for a single opera but, particularly in smaller cities, it is more common to use them to shift around the various complete operas between rehearsal and performance. The availability of rehearsal stages certainly simplifies fitting up, since parts of scenes are likely to have been built already for rehearsal and construction snags discovered.

Backstage in one of the smaller German opera houses. The lighting equipment is mounted on a bridge and tower structure so that it is accessible for focusing between, or even during, scenes. The bridge and tower form a false proscenium which is adjustable to the size required for a particular production.

Lighting

There are two methods of dealing with lighting in a repertoire theatre. Both are based on a permanent rig, for there is no time to hang any but the very simplest essential extra bars or booms. One system, particularly favoured in the Central European theatres of the German tradition, uses a relatively small number of spotlights mounted on access bridges, towers and galleries. These are manned by a large permanent trained lighting staff who refocus and angle some of the spotlights in scene changes and also follow the singers with others. When the repertoire is large, there may be a couple of weeks between performances of a particular work and it can be difficult for singers to be absolutely precise in taking up stage positions. Also, substitute singers may have to go on with limited rehearsal. All this is easier to cope with when the lights are manned. German opera houses have an adjustable false proscenium which carries horizontal bridges and vertical towers: these bridges and towers move with the proscenium when it is adjusted to give the appropriate height and width to frame a scene. Grids are much higher so that borders are rarely needed for masking and are only introduced if required for decoration. This means that a three-tier lighting bridge can reach all positions upstage while maintaining a good lighting angle.

The alternative system is a *saturation rig* which, as its name implies, crams the maximum number of spotlights possible into the theatre, both FOH and backstage. These spots are classified in three ways: (1) permanently focused for a systematic general coverage, (2) focused as specials for particular productions and locked-off in these positions, and (3) re-focused daily as required. The selection required to meet the needs of a particular production is made at a patch panel or by cross-plugging at the socket boxes feeding the various lighting positions. The latest control systems, pioneered at London's National Theatre, make the selection as part of the memory programme for each production.

Where the theatre building permits an on-stage bridge and towers, there is a lot to be said in favour of a compromise system using a reasonably large number of lanterns with a small attendant staff. Certainly the standard procedures of the straight play are no use—there is no time to set up Act II Sc 4 in the afternoon just to focus a couple of spotlights. Yet this scene may arrive in a 60-second musical scene change. No time for ladders! And the set only needs to be slightly off its marks (stretched stage cloth?) for a spotlight shuttered into a window to make a nasty splodge: a moment when there is no real substitute for a man on a bridge.

Some opera companies lay out numbered canvas strips at right angles to one another along the centre and setting lines. These act as co-ordinates for a grid system of plotting the light beam positions on an empty stage. During changeovers the spotlights can then be set quickly before the scenery is built because a tallescope ladder can be wheeled easily to all parts of the empty stage. The system works well for general coverage but precision shutterings have to be checked after the scenery is set.

It should be emphasised that the procedures of lighting preparation and rehearsal are exactly the same as those described for play and musical except for the disciplines imposed by consideration of, and respect for, the needs of other works in the repertoire.

Stage management

The prompt book in an opera house is an interleaved copy of the vocal score and the cues are marked to be given on specific notes in specific bars. Opera stage management have to know enough about musical notation to be able to make up and read this kind of musical prompt copy. It is just not possible to take cues from words or actions. In opera, the timing is controlled by the conductor and not by the actors: in most cases the music cannot wait for a missed cue in the way that actors can ad lib or vary the pace so that a late scenic movement can catch up. Opera cues are therefore given precisely with the music, watching the stage only to check safety and perhaps to integrate the type of cue sequence where a cloth must be dropped in before the lights are brought up. It is customary in opera for a member of the stage management staff (not the one in the corner, running the show) to check that the singers are ready for entrances and sometimes to cue them on. Backstage, in addition to normal stage management cueing, there is likely to be at least one member of the music staff to conduct off-stage choruses, bands, drum-rolls, etc.

Prompting is also a province of the music staff rather than the stage management. Because the orchestral accompaniment keeps going on when a singer forgets a line, prompting after the event is too late. Prompting has to be in advance and, as it is difficult to tell just when a singer is going to dry, every line has to be hissed out by the prompter from his little box in the centre of the footlights. As opera houses become regarded more and more as musical theatre, the services of a prompter tend to be considered unnecessary. However, an opera house always needs prompt box facilities to use in emergencies such as sudden cast replacements due to illness.

Piano dress rehearsal

The key staging rehearsal is the piano dress. Hopefully, individual scenes will already have been tackled on stage with scenery and props. Now the whole opera is put together: singers, costumes, props, lights, effects, etc. The only missing element is the orchestra. The piano dress is the final production rehearsal to belong exclusively to the director. The singers concentrate on production problems and only occasionally open out vocally. Although music takes a back seat, it is to be hoped that the conductor will take part rather than send a deputy. An opera conductor has rather more to do than in the concert hall: there is a lot of integration required between pit and production, particularly on exits and entrances, and at the beginnings and ends of scenes. The piano dress is the time to get all this straight, for this is the last rehearsal at which it will be possible to stop and go back for anything other than musical problems. Opera rehearsals are generally in three hour sessions and a piano dress will normally be allocated two such sessions to allow time for stopping to clear up problems. As always by this point in rehearsals, it is the stage manager who must get the rehearsal re-started after a stop: in this case by cueing the conductor.

(*overleaf*) The weekly schedule for the Summer Opera Festival at Glyndebourne is circulated several months before the first rehearsal. Amendments to update this spiral-bound schedule book are issued regularly and a daily schedule is issued every afternoon with a detailed breakdown for the following day.

COL			THURSDAY 26	FRIDAY 27	SATURDAY 28	SUNDAY 29
1	T H E A T R E	M	10.30-1.30 Vixen w.o.			
		A	2.30-4p.m. Vixen w.o. 4.15-5.30 Voix o.a.	2.00-5p.m. 2 x Don w.o./C/ Light	2.00-5p.m. 1 x Vixen wo/C Lights	
		E	Tech	6-9p.m.	6.30-7.15p.m. Voix sitz w.o. 7.30-9.30p.m. Voix w.o.	5.30 DON FINAL REH.
2	R E H E A R S A L (STAGE)	M	2 x Falstaff w.p.	2 x Falstaff w.p.	2 x Falstaff w.p.	2 x Falstaff w.p.
		A				
		E				
3	P R O D U C T I O N	M	1 x Don underst. w.p.	1 x Vixen underst. w.p.	1 x Don underst. w.p.	1 x Don underst. w.p.
		T				1 x Vixen underst. w.p.
		E				
4	M U S I C	M			S. Frau mus.	S. Frau mus.
		A			W. Davis	W. Davis
		E				
5	N.A.		Peters Lott	Braithwaite fr. 5pm Allen Matheson-Bruce fr 5pm Cannan	Braithwaite Plowright Peters Matheson-Bruce Gottlieb J.	
6	ARRIVE				Davis	
7	DEPART				Isepp (to June 13)	Fraser
8	NOTES		Matheson- Bruce on recall ENO	Stage I pm II eve Phillips eve	Matheson-Bruce on recall ENO	

REHEARSAL SCHEDULE - SUNDAY MAY 29th

STAGE: 5.30 for 5.40   DON GIOVANNI F.R.

REHEARSAL   10.30-1.30   )
STAGE: 10pm - 12 midnight)   FALSTAFF Production Rehearsal

HECTOR: 10.30-1.30   DON GIOVANNI Production Rehearsal (Understudies)
                3.00-5.00   VIXEN   Production Rehearsal

DON GIOVANNI F.R.:   PRITCHARD
                                                               HALL
5.30 for 5.40   ACT I: Dean, Luxon, Carden, Andrade,   MALLANDAINE
                            Goeke, Thau, Rawnsley, Gale,   CLEOBURY
                            FULL CHORUS, Supers   WILDER
                                                               PETER-SZABO
7.10 approx.   LONG INTERVAL

8.25 for 8.35   ACT II CAST as above, MENS CHORUS,
                            Supers, Richards.

ALL PRINCIPALS IN DRESSING ROOMS 1 HOUR BEFORE FIRST APPEARANCE PLEASE

1.30-9.45pm   GREEN ROOM RESERVED AS A QUIET REST ROOM

Warm-ups   11.00   Carden   PETER-SZABO   Louise
            4.15   Luxon   MALLANDAINE   Rehearsal Stage
            4.45   Andrade   "
            5.10   Gale   "   "   "   "

                    Production Rehearsal Understudies   Hector
10.30   Plowright, Rath, M. Lewis   TROTTER
11.30   Plowright, Rath, K. Lewis, Harrhy   FRASER
12.30   Plowright, Harrhy, K. Lewis, M. Lewis, Rath
1.00   Price joins

VIXEN: 3.00-5.00   Production Rehearsal   Hector

3.00   Cannan, Flowers, M-Bruce, Korman, Herford   VICK
4.30   McKinnon joins   WARD
                                                               FRASER
                    Musical Rehearsals

10.30-12.00   Herford   WARD   Ptolemy
12.15-1.30   Nemeer   WARD   Ptolemy

FALSTAFF: 10.30-1.30   ) Production Rehearsal
                10pm-12midnight)   Rehearsal Stage
                                                              PONNELLE eve.
11.30-1.30 I/1 Capecchi, (Kerry), Trama Dickerson,   HOPE (PRITCHARD)
                 Nemeer, Fryatt, Page-boy   BRADSHAW
                                                              WILDER a.m.
10p.m.-12 midnight Capecchi, Ellis   MALLANDAINE eve

SCHWEIGSAME FRAU   10.30-1.30) Ensemble   Organ Room
                    2.30-5.30)   DAVIS, HINDEN
10.30   Peters, Gottlieb, Cross   BRAITHWAITE
11.00-1.30)   Cast by arrangement after Saturday   (FIFIELD) BEALa.m.
2.30-5.30)   evening rehearsal.   BARLOW a.m.
                                                              (WILDER)
2.30-3.30   Peters   BEAL, BARLOW   Conductor's Room
3.45-5.00   Summerscales   BEAL   Conductor's Room
3.45-5.00   Cannan   BARLOW   Ptolemy

CHORUS: 4.55   DON GIOVANNI FULL CHORUS Warm-up Lily Davis Room
                5.30 for 5.40   DON GIOVANNI F.R.

N.A.:   Brodie, Bowman, Davia

CATERING   The Staff Restaurant will be open 12.30-2.00 & Long Interval - NO
                                      GUESTS PLEASE

Sitzprobe

After the orchestra have had their own rehearsals, they meet up with the singers at a session called the *sitzprobe*. This is a purely musical rehearsal with, traditionally, a row of chairs set out at the front of the stage for the singers. Sometimes, particularly in theatres with an inclination to view opera rather more as music theatre, this rehearsal takes the form of a 'walking sitzprobe' where singers move about to take up their approximate stage positions. The stage management find the sitzprobe useful for getting accustomed to following the prompt score while listening to the orchestral sound after weeks of rehearsal piano.

Orchestral dress rehearsals

As indicated earlier, orchestral dress rehearsals are to be regarded primarily as musical rehearsals. It is the role of the director and technical staff to keep quiet and make notes unless real problems occur and they are forced or asked to intervene. As always, the stage manager is in charge but he would only halt the rehearsal in the event of danger or a really major technical problem. Otherwise stops should only be for musical reasons. Some stops will be for off-stage music: there is nothing quite like a distant trumpet call for bringing an entire opera house to a grinding halt. Other stops will be about difficulties in seeing the conductor, and the director may have to rearrange moves and positions. Whether to amend or whether to hold out for a further attempt to make the original ideas work requires a fine degree of judgement of how real the problem is. Moments like this soon show up how well the director and conductor have worked together on a joint conception.

After these dress rehearsals, two types of note session may be required: production and musical. Any time remaining at the end of the three-hour orchestral session is used to go back over balance or ensemble problems. Individual problems are usually dealt with in special coaching sessions. Director's notes have to be given in rehearsal room as the stage must be made available for changeover to the evening performance.

General rehearsal

The final rehearsal before the opening performance is called the *general* and is sometimes played, rather in the nature of a preview, to an invited audience. Rehearsals for a new production place quite a strain on voices and it is customary to have the general 48 hours before the opening performance to allow a full day's rest in between.

Revivals

Much of the foregoing discussion has been about the introduction of new productions into the repertoire. This may be the more exciting part of the work but the standing of an opera

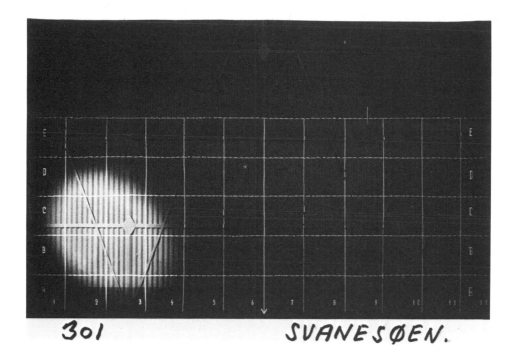

301   SVANESØEN.

house and its obligations to its audience depend upon maintaining the standard of productions for as long as they remain in
the repertoire and on their subsequent revival. The staging
standards of a production are kept up to scratch by a staff
director who was probably assistant director during the original
mounting of the opera. This staff director watches all performances and rehearses any cast changes. When the opera is
revived in future seasons, he acts as director if the original
director is not available or not willing to rehearse the revival in
person.

Plans and plots of all kinds must be particularly detailed as
operas which have been out of the repertoire for a considerable
time, even years, get revived with minimum technical rehearsal.
Photographic records are particularly useful checks of scenery
and prop settings and some opera houses file *progress shot*
photographs showing move-by-move sequences of actor group-
ings.

At the Royal Opera in
Copenhagen, the position
of each front-of-house
spotlight is recorded by
photographing its image on
the fire-curtain. This
enables the lights to be
focused for the evening
performance while the
scenery is being assembled
behind the lowered safety
curtain.

Temperament

It is popularly thought that opera singers are very tem-
peramental. Not true—the reverse is the case. Opera singers
have to continue to study and practise their technique throughout their careers and, in the author's experience, often demon-
strate a far more professional approach to their work than many
performers in other branches of theatre.

13 Staging the dance

It is logical to consider ballet immediately after opera since they both perform in repertoire and they often share the same stage. An opera house can supply two basic needs of ballet: a big stage and a big orchestra. Or at least these were the basic requirements until the recent development of modern dance companies playing in any kind of performance space from the large formal proscenium stage to the informal studio area, and preferring tape or chamber ensemble to the traditional full orchestra. However, whatever the scale, there are certain common problems to all modes of dance staging.

Scenery

The basis of the dance repertoire is short single-act works and it is even quite common for programmes to include single acts selected from the relatively small number of available full-length ballets. So there is quite a lot of interval in a dance evening: four acts and three intervals are quite usual and the intervals have to be longish to allow the dancers to recover and do a complete costume and possibly make-up change. This means that there is not usually a time problem with interval scene changes. Many one-act ballets have no changes within the act and where there is a change it is often just a simple fly cue (although there are, as always, exceptions—'Petroushka' for example, depends on slick major changes). So the main scenic problems are those associated with the daily round of rehearsal and performance. This is further complicated because an evening's programme may be made up from various combinations of the available one-act repertoire. Two short works which have always been simple may suddenly become a problem when played together on the same evening. However, most dance scenery is technically straightforward. The dancers basically require a flat stage area so there is a distinct lack of the rostra and steps to give the levels that other theatre forms demand. The standard form is backcloth and wings, and many short pieces are done with only a backcloth and plain black wings. The big classics make full use of backcloths, gauzes and limited built scenery. The quality of the stage floor is very important, both in smoothness and springiness. Special vinyl floor coverings are available and these can be rolled for touring.

Lighting

Most ballets require good overall coverage in a choice of colour washes with lots of side lighting to sculpture the dancers' bodies and emphasise the dimensional quality of their limb movements. This is generally supplied by a spot bar upstage of each border for top light, and a tower upstage of each wing for side lighting. Towers are generally preferred to conventional booms or ladders as they can be moved upstage or downstage in act changes to adjust to the varying positions of wing flats. The towers consist of a heavily weighted wheeled base supporting a

Portable lighting towers form a useful method of side lighting dancers.

vertical boom of about 12 or 14 feet in height. The resultant light is close to horizontal and this is a good angle for limb lighting. To avoid shadows being cast on the wings at the opposite side of the stage, the wings are angled so that the onstage edge is very slightly downstage. From the front, the wing looks parallel to the front of the stage but the slight angle stops it from receiving shadows.

It is difficult to colour hanging lighting equipment during an interval change but it can and has been done. Most companies, however, keep static colours in the overhead lights and change the filters for each act in the more accessible side lighting. Because the emphasis is on body movement rather than facial expression, dance tends to use less FOH lighting than other forms of theatre.

Follow spots are sometimes used to emphasise the soloists but a single conventional follow spot is very flattening to the dancer's movements. If follow spots are used, there should be at least two, possibly three, from angles appropriate to dimensional sculpturing.

Some modern choreography has sequences which do not use the whole stage but involve almost stationary dancers using only subtle movements. For this, selective area lighting is appropriate and such works tend to have many more cues than the more open full-stage style of ballets.

Organisation

Staging organisation is not unlike that of an opera company; ballet companies resident in opera houses generally share all the opera's technical facilities and most of the staff except stage management. Dancers have the most extensive schedules of all performing artists, including daily class as well as rehearsals for performances. This needs extensive planning, and when rehearsal rooms are not available on tour the technical work of the stage has to be organised to leave the stage free for rehearsal during as much of the day as possible, even if this involves overnight technical work. Fortunately many of the settings are so simple that comparatively little time is required for daily changeover.

14 Staging
light entertainment

The expression *light entertainment* is not intended to imply that the forms of theatre discussed in previous chapters are heavy and serious. Nor is this chapter going to be about colour music, light shows, son et lumière or any of the other types of entertainment dependent on fluid light rather than actors. Light entertainment is a useful television classification for a group of types of show for which there is no collective theatre term. The group includes revue, variety, pantomime, and to put it rather basically, any forms of show that are put together with scissors and paste. The basis of these shows is that varying amounts of the performance material (script, music, props, costumes, etc.) are supplied by the performers themselves in a ready-made rehearsed form. A light entertainment show is compiled rather than written; it consists of a series of *acts* joined together by *production*. The proportion of specially written material included with the acts and the degree to which the acts are integrated into the production varies according to the type of show.

Variety (Vaudeville)

A true variety bill is a series of self-contained acts without any linking material between them. After the applause at the end of one act, the orchestra go straight into the music of the next act. This immediate musical join is called a *segue* and the term is used a lot in theatre jargon (usually emphasised as *dead segue*) to describe any immediate follow on. Variety bills are only occasionally performed in theatres nowadays. Variety has completed a full cycle from pub through music hall and variety theatre to club where its acts play to an audience again seated at refreshment tables.

Variety acts are complete mini-productions. They have their

own scripts, music, costumes and props (variety actors are usually called *artistes* and they use the word 'props' to cover both props and wardrobe). The only item that they do not carry is scenery, relying on the resident stage manager to provide a suitable background. Among the sadly disappearing traditional arts and crafts of the theatre is the ingenuity with which the resident stage managers decorated their stages week after week with every conceivable combination and permutation of stock drapes. Artists normally construct their acts so that the closing section can be performed downstage to allow the indispensable tabs ('No 1 runners') to be closed behind them to allow the next act to set their props and for any scene change to be carried out.

Variety artists write their lighting plots (on the backs of box-office advertising cards) in terms of the colour washes produced by red, blue and white battens and floats, with limes assumed to be in use unless specified otherwise. The possibilities are:

Full up	Blackout
Red Stage	Pin Focus
Blue Stage	FUF
Colours	Iris Out

Most of these are obvious. 'Pin focus', usually asked for with a blackout, means a tight lime (head only). There are two ways of ending a musical number: 'FUF' (standing for full-up-finish) meaning build up to full over last bar(s) of music to get applause, and 'iris out' meaning slowly fade everything towards the end of the number with the lime irising smaller and smaller and finally out on the last note—count 2, 3 and UP full for applause. No cues are given from the prompt corner: the cue positions are marked on the plot and the lighting operator takes them himself by listening to the act. It is also assumed that the operator will listen to and 'feel' the music, so no cue timings in seconds are written into the plot.

The traditional variety rehearsal is (or sadly, one almost has to say 'was') the Monday band call. On arrival at the theatre, the acts put their band parts on the footlights to establish a 'first come first served' rota to have their music rehearsed by the resident musical director (MD), special attention being given to tempi, cues and drummer's effects. While awaiting their turn with the band, the actors unpack their props and confer with the resident stage manager and chief electrician about scenic and lighting requirements. The key document is the running order, showing the times allotted to each act, and the resident stage manager is responsible for ensuring at each performance that the individual acts do not over-run.

When the acts perform in clubs a similar rehearsal routine is obviously required but there is a tendency for the call to be rather more informal and, except in the big clubs, for the staff to be rather less experienced and possibly less professional in their approach.

A typical lighting plot for a variety act.

Handwritten lighting plot:

Billy Crockett's 2ᴺᴰ Spot

Trumpet	Colours + FUF
Small Sax	F.U.
Gloves	Bowf + FUF
Piano	F.U.
Rest of the World Go By	Dark Colours
Dark Town Strutters Ball	Blues + FUF
Post Horn Galop	Bowf + Fuf
Saw	Colours + FUF
Concertina	Dark Colours + FUF

Note — Limes White Focus All Through

Revue

The term *revue* is used to cover a multitude of theatre forms from intimate satire to spectacular diversion. Some forms of revue, compiled from original songs, dances and sketches, are really musicals and are staged as such. The more common form of revue is a mixture of musical and variety. The format is usually a sequence of production scenes interspersed with variety acts. Some of the big spectaculars in places like Las Vegas run for years with regular changes in the featured acts.

In British seaside holiday resorts, the summer revue starring television personalities is the standard entertainment. The average run is only 10–12 weeks but the scenery and costumes for the production numbers can be moved each summer to a different town allowing production costs to be spread over several years. The production numbers are staged with identical techniques to those employed in staging a musical but with emphasis on visual splendour. Costumes and scenery must appear lavish with the lighting bold, contrasty and colourful. Gauzes must melt away and scenery must move like magic. There is no room for any kind of visual restraint. The acts must be dovetailed into the production so that the joins do not show. Dancers and singers may be used to provide an introduction. Special scenery is often provided for the acts and their music re-orchestrated to fit the style of the show's band. The act's red, blue and FUF plots have to be interpreted in terms of the show's lighting rig which is likely to be rather more extensive than the average variety theatre or club. In fact a variety lighting plot contains all the vital information if red and blue are translated as warm and cool; colours can be interpreted as 'pretty' and full up means bright rather than every single light on at full. Blackout usually does mean blackout; but blackout with pin focus lime might just possibly include just a touch of backlight or a hint of blue on the cyclorama. The electrics department in a revue usually has to cope, in addition to normal lighting, with all sorts of practicals including star cloths and hundreds of bulbs wired to switch on and off in sequence as 'chasers'.

The main problem in setting and striking—and this is particularly true of summer shows—is musical acts with large drum kits, several keyboards and an assortment of guitar amplifiers. Lengthy front cloth scenes often have to be incorporated into the running order before and after. It helps if most of the gear can be mounted on a truck but many summer theatres have, to put it mildly, restricted wing space.

Pantomime

The Christmas pantomime is a unique British institution (possibly our only truly indigenous theatre form) and this is certainly not the place to attempt to explain its construction and conventions. It frequently has the technical complexities of a full major musical but it is rehearsed and staged in a fraction of the time. Pantomime scenery is not quite immortal but it is expected to be still showing considerable life after twenty years or so of annual Christmas seasons. In its declining years it tends to get cut down and may be used for a quite different story subject. As it gets older, increasingly stronger gels are required in the lights to revive its fading charms. The panto pump is primed each year by a couple or so new shows which start in number one theatres and move outwards then downwards to a different theatre each year. The stars not only interpolate their own speciality acts but insert songs, chunks of dialogue, and even complete scenes to suit their own particular talents. Keeping the story line reasonably intact is not easy but it is important as pantomime is often a child's first encounter with theatre—which also means keeping technical standards very high although this is not always easy with a long season of twice daily performances.

The biggest single staging problem is keeping the show to its scheduled running time. If a pantomime is found at its first performance to run too long, the number and complexity of scene and costume changes can make cuts incredibly difficult to insert. One cut can introduce a whole sequence of difficulties. Stopwatch timing of every section of dialogue and music is therefore essential. Even the biggest and newest pantos rarely get more than two weeks in the rehearsal room followed by a week on stage. This means only three evenings of dress rehearsal which is very tight for a big musical production full of transformation scenes. However, if the sections are worked on independently by day—and the structure of a pantomime lends itself to lots of sectional rehearsals going on concurrently—the evening dress rehearsals can be used for polishing the joins.

The department needing most organisation may well be props because much of the comedy is visual and the comics are

In fast shows, it is often easier for the stage manager to call the cues from a list rather than from a conventional prompt book.

	Act I
	WARN ELEX, TABS. + FLYS
	HOUSE TO ½ }
	CONDUCTOR GO }
(FINALE THEME)	HOUSE OUT
	TAPE GO
(TINP ROLE)	HOUSE TABS OUT
	ELEX 1
(FAIRY ON)	ELEX 2
	FLYS 1 (BLACKS)
(BLEED WITH OBOE)	ELEX 3
	FLYS 2 (GAULE)
	ELEX 4
(BOYS LIFT DL.)	ELEX 5
	CALL DAME
	WARN ELEX 6 — 9
(ENTRANCE)	ELEX 6
(PATTER)	ELEX 7
(KIPPER GAG)	LINE TO GREEN
	LINE RESTORE
(INTO NUMBER)	ELEX 8
(UP TEMPO)	ELEX 9
	CHECK DRESSER STANDING BY.
(FUF)	ELEX 10
	WARN ELEX (11—17) FLYS (3+4)
	No 1 RUNNERS, SMOKE, PS STAR TRAP
(WITCH ON)	ELEX 11 }
	FLYS 3 }
	SMOKE }
	TRAP }

dependent on props, many of which are quite intricate. Because of the short staging time, it is even more true than usual that the show can only be as good as the quality of the homework done by the director and production manager.

Stage managing light entertainment

Obviously most light entertainment productions have no bound printed scripts, although pantomimes usually have copies of the dialogue liberally sprinkled with blank spaces for items like 'dame's spot' and 'ghost gag'. A revue prompt copy can and should be made by bringing together such individual scripts as exist for sketches, lyrics, etc. But for running the show it is probably better to work from a detailed running order showing all the fly, stage, tab, lighting, effects cues in the sequence that they are given. In any theatre form where there is a lot of ad-libbing, the important line is the *tag* that triggers the blackout and sets off a whole sequence of cues.

The importance of keeping to time has been indicated and it is customary for the stage manager to log detailed timings of individual sequences in far greater detail than with a play. Any divergence from agreed timings must be brought to the immediate attention of the performer concerned.

15 Staging tours

Very broadly speaking, three types of production go on tour: specially staged *touring productions*, prior to London or Broadway *try-outs*, and normally resident repertoire companies on their *annual tour*.

Tours play in two types of venue: the standard *touring circuit* of theatres whose main product is the touring show and whose staff are accustomed to dealing with its problems, and the *secondary circuit* of miscellaneous halls with small and/or inexperienced staffs. A production specially staged for touring is budgeted and designed to take into account the special circumstances of touring, whereas try-outs and annual tours are special cases. Let us, therefore, start with a consideration of the standard situation of a touring production on the touring circuit.

Scheduling the get in

The standard tour is based on stop-overs in each theatre of one week or, occasionally, multiples of one week. Consequently the total time available for getting out, travelling and getting in to the next date is from the Saturday fall of the curtain until its rise on Monday. Transport of scenery in Britain is now entirely by road. Movement by rail finished after the 1950s for a number of reasons. First, the railways withdrew the traditional free truck concessions for companies travelling their actors by train. Then they could no longer guarantee nationwide delivery by late Sunday or early Monday. And finally the door-to-door convenience of road haulage with its reduction in both wear and tear on the scenery and the labour costs of its handling (loading and unloading are required only at the theatre rather than at both theatre and station as in the old days).

Unless the move is a particularly long distance one like Aberdeen to Bournemouth, the Sunday get-in can be at

2 pm—on many journeys, 9 am is possible. Simple shows, particularly standing set plays, can get-in on a Monday but this is tight scheduling and is dependent on the theatres being able to supply enough staff. Touring theatres have small permanent staffs and rely on a pool of part-time casuals for getting the shows in and out at the weekends, and working on the evening performances if there are scene changes. Many of these casuals have worked every weekend for years and are frequently more experienced than many full time theatre technicians. The problem is that many of them are not available during the day on a Monday although some theatres have casual staffs that include workers—often milkmen, postmen or railmen—who can adjust their working hours to be available at tricky times like Monday get-ins and Wednesday matinees.

A Monday get-in is attractive because it is cheaper. The details of whether 'them' or 'us' are responsible for payment of staff are defined in the contract but the general custom is that the theatre pays for a reasonable number of men to get the show in on a Monday while the touring company pays for the get-out at the end of the week. The cost of any Sunday work is shared equally between theatre and tour. Sunday work, being at double time, is expensive. A frequent compromise is to work the minimum call of four hours on Sunday. This allows everything to be unloaded, the lighting hung, and the basic set erected. The cost of the Sunday call is often offset by a better deal with the haulage company who like to get their vehicles unloaded on a Sunday and back to base.

Touring theatres are being used increasingly on Sundays for concerts and other forms of one night stand performance, and so the only stage work possible is unloading and perhaps some hanging. If the show is particularly heavy, it may be necessary to work overnight after the concert.

Touring staff

The only non-acting staff toured by the simplest plays are the stage management: a stage manager doubling as company manager, a deputy SM to run the corner and at least one ASM (but preferably two) to cope with props and sound effects. As the form of the show grows more complex there is first a touring carpenter and then an electrician added. With musicals the practice of carrying a sound operator has been increasing in recent years. The carpenter and electrician are required only at weekends so it is quite usual for them to go home on Tuesday mornings and reappear on Saturday afternoons.

Resident staff calls

The touring theatre provides the number of staff requested by the manager of the touring company. There are two different numbers involved: the number of staff required to run the performances and the number required to get the show in. The number of staff to get the show out is always the same as the number to get it in—an old custom now formalised in union agreements. As a result, the touring manager's responsibility for paying the cost of the get-out acts as a brake on the number of men called for the get-in, even though the theatre picks up the wages bill for the get-in. In fact, judging the ideal number of staff required is a finely balanced compromise between too few and so many that they get in each other's way. Furthermore, there are few one-theatre towns that can lay on, say, eight casual experienced theatre electricians.

The *staff call* is the touring company's main advance contact with the backstage staff and is a key link in the formation of a good 'us' and 'them' relationship. The quality of these calls has fallen off in recent years (it is not unknown for the resident stage manager to have to telephone the touring company at the eleventh hour to discover their requirements, even their proposed arrival time).

The main points in calling are:

* Send the call in writing to the resident stage manager and the chief electrician at least 10 days in advance.

* The larger the staff required, the longer should be the notice.

* Follow up with a telephone call two or three days before get-in to check that there are no problems. When there is a touring carpenter and/or electrician, they should make these phone calls to their opposite numbers.

* Never send calls via the theatre manager: they nearly always get no further than the front office filing tray.

* Give the time of the call.

* Indicate the likely length of any Sunday calls.

* Give the number of staff in each department required for (a) get-in and (b) performance.

* Give the number as 'chief plus' or 'HOD plus' to avoid confusion as to whether head of department is included in the number or not.

Colour call

Another important call is the colour call which lists the colour filters required in the theatre's lighting equipment (the touring company carry any filters required by their own equipment). This should be sent at the same time as the staff call along with a note of special electrical requirements.

Production weekend

The first weekend of a tour is rather similar to any other kind of staging weekend except that a Tuesday opening is extremely unlikely. There should be a stopping dress rehearsal on the Sunday evening and a dress reheasal on the Monday afternoon. In the case of very simple plays, the Sunday rehearsal may take the form of a run-through in working light. This saves money as the only staff required is a stand-by electrician. There should not be a Sunday concert on a production weekend but it can happen and this of course wipes out the possibility of a Sunday rehearsal unless overnight Saturday working is included: this is fine for a prior-to-London try-out but is usually beyond the budget of a routine commercial tour.

Many tours are re-cast versions of Broadway or London successes using the original scenery and props. Sometimes the scenery is simplified: sets have been known to shed their ceilings after the first week of such a tour. Lighting is usually simplified so that it can be adapted to use the local equipment wherever possible. Vital extra lanterns are carried but most British touring theatres (often with Arts Council aid) now have a sufficient stock of lights to meet most touring needs. The situation is different in America where it is normal to tour a complete lighting rig including dimmer boards.

The question of setting line is a little tricky in touring theatres because of variations in apron depth and the space taken up by permanent tormentors, tabs, screens, etc., immediately upstage of the proscenium. The best solution is to strike the setting line in relation to the theatre's No. 1 spot bar: it will then be possible to focus the lighting to the same areas each week. However the sightlines in a particular theatre in relation to a particular show have to be borne in mind and it is a matter for discussion between touring and resident stage managers.

An important weekly ritual of touring is the Monday morning visit of the local fire prevention officer who will ask questions about naked flames, pyrotechnic effects, etc. He will also apply his lighter to check the fireproofing of potentially risky materials like gauzes and window curtains. His attitude in tricky circumstances will reflect his confidence in the resident stage manager, but the fire regulations are on the whole good sound commonsense and no one in their right mind would wish to 'get round' them.

Quite often there will be a carpenter and lighting designer in attendance for the production weekend only: they will put up the set and light it. Whenever possible the touring stage manager should watch them like a hawk to see how they do it. However, he is likely to be called away to the telephone or to sort out prop and wardrobe problems etc. He should ensure that he is left with proper plans and plots for both scenery and lights and he should talk through these with the specialists before they leave. During the first week the stage manager should ensure that all parts of the scenery are correctly and clearly marked and he should have all the spotlights flashed out to see exactly where they have been focused. It is worthwhile having a chat with the resident stage manager about any tricky parts of the fit up, including the best order in which to carry out certain operations.

Change-over weekends

After the first week, there are normally no weekend rehearsals: the show is got in, up and lit. The last item, the lighting, should finish by 5 pm latest on the Monday but it is not unknown for the last cue to be plotted as the half hour is being called. Touring theatre staffs are geared to working 'cold' without technical rehearsal but they rely on the touring stage management being particularly calm and clear in their cueing. The success of Monday night depends on gearing the production to the 'art of the possible' and creatively adapting to local conditions.

Get-out

The dismantling of the show and loading into transport for the move to the next date is known as the *get-out* (*load out* in America, *bump out* in Australia). Payment for the get-out (i.e. for all work on the show carried out after the fall of the final curtain on Saturday night) is a lump sum per man negotiated in advance by the heads of the theatre's technical departments with the touring manager and based on an estimate of the difficulty of the work and the likely time required to complete it. Traditionally, to ensure that the work was done properly, the get-out was not paid until loading was completed. However, a combination of the responsibility of modern staffs and the complexity of modern accounting systems has brought about a change in such time-hallowed customs. The art of getting out is, not surprisingly, dismantling in the correct order, packing securely, and not leaving anything behind.

Gratuities

It is customary for the touring company to show their appreciation for the work of the resident technical staff by making a small disbursement. This is usually referred to as a 'drink' but normally takes cash form. The small touring companies, travelling without specialist staff, are often particularly dependent on the local staff beyond the call of contractual duty. In small companies gratuities are disbursed by the touring company manager, in larger ones by the heads of the technical departments. The distribution of the total sum should not be fixed but should vary from week to week to reflect the degree of helpfulness of the various individual technicians.

Try-outs

There are two kinds of tours billed as *prior to London*. There are those with a commitment, including finance, for a West End opening on a certain date. And there are those who travel hopefully. The hopeful tours are try-outs in the literal sense: the purpose of touring being to test the show before an audience to find out if it has the potential to become a 'hit', perhaps with re-writing and re-casting. There is not usually enough finance available for a West End run: the hope is that with sufficient evidence of potential success, the necessary backing will be forthcoming. The hopeful tour is now on the decline: this kind of try-out is now more likely to take the form of a three-week run in a regional repertory company. When a hopeful try-out does take to the road, it does so in a way similar to any standard tour.

However, a committed prior-to-London tour is somewhat different. The purpose is to put a final polish on the show by playing to an audience in the evenings while continuing some rehearsal by day. Technically, there is an attempt to reproduce the conditions that will eventually apply in the London theatre and there is much less adaptation to local conditions than with a normal tour. The sets tend to be more complex than normal touring sets and the lighting will, as nearly as possible, be a replica of that to be used in the London theatre. All this requires more staff, more time, more transport and these add up to more money. In theory some of this extra expenditure should be offset by more box office income generated by a glamorously-cast new production but in practice the prior-to label has been so ill-used in the past that regional audiences can be more than a little suspicious until word-of-mouth confirms the worth of the show. As a result, in budgeting such a tour, it is usually necessary to consider some of the touring expenses as production rather than running costs: the tour is part of an investment in eventual success.

Unless the production is a play of the very simplest type, the first week should open on a Tuesday. And an overnight get-in immediately following the get-out of the previous week's show is quite frequent. Subsequent weeks may open on a Monday but will need a full Sunday's technical work.

In the case of musical try-outs there may only be a couple of touring dates, or even just one, and the whole production team is likely to stay with the show for most of the tour as this often involves substitution of new musical numbers and changes in running order. The changes are often made at short notice and introduce more complications for the technical staff than for the actors. Unsuccessful changes are partially restored—such restoration often being more technically difficult that the original cut! Eventually the plots consist mainly of Scotch tape. It is necessary to 'freeze' the show for the last couple of performances in one date and the first in the next to permit a smooth weekend move.

Annual tours

Many national companies are based on biggish stages, so there is a size problem when they take to the road. Sets need to be adapted and this can be done to some extent by simply leaving out bits. The big opera companies sometimes build simplified versions of their sets using a combination of original and special pieces. Smaller cloths may be required. This is not as expensive a way of mounting a touring production as it sounds (in relation to total costs) because the original costumes and smaller props can be used without modification and very little special rehearsal is required. The touring lighting rig consists of a simplified version of the basic repertoire installation in the home theatre. Such tours, whether drama, opera or dance, usually present a repertoire of up to three or four programmes, the more popular productions being played for perhaps two or three performances during the week with the less popular only once. These companies tour a sizeable staff drawn from their experienced home base personnel. The success of the operation depends basically on the degree of imaginative skill with which the tour staging staff can adapt to local conditions, trying to follow the spirit rather than the detail of the original production.

Secondary touring circuit

This discussion on touring has been assuming a circuit of conventional touring theatres having, as minimum, a proscenium stage with fly tower and an experienced technical staff of at least five or six plus the possibility of calling upon a pool of experienced casual part-time showmen for evening performances and weekend changeovers.

At the other end of the scale there is the *fit-up tour* which carries everything and assumes nothing. Such a tour does not rely on finding flying space or even a suspension grid above the stage. The company is self-sufficient in that it can mount the show in virtually any kind of building without the assistance of any skilled local staff.

In between there is a *secondary circuit* consisting mainly of multi-purpose civic halls plus some university theatres and repertory theatres, taking in a few weeks of touring between seasons of the resident company. These stages include every possible variation in size, shape and facilities. If they have any common feature, it is a tendency to have very wide proscenium openings coupled with insufficient depth. Flying facilities vary from the full to the token. The staff can be enthusiastic rather than experienced, although occasionally the enthusiasm is tempered by an excess of respect for bureaucratic procedures. There is very rarely a pool of experienced showmen on hand. The lighting equipment has a habit of being inflexible and inaccessible. One cannot depend on finding either a clear grid or a clear stage: many such things which are taken for granted in the main touring theatre circuit have to be asked for specifically.

If the touring show's technical requirements are anything other than very basic, an advance 'recce' visit will cover its cost several times over. Any problems tend to be a simple matter of communication and one has to recognise that the big theatre practice of quick phone calls in jargon will not work for unorthodox buildings staffed by enthusiasts who may not have worked anywhere else but have found out how to solve the problems of their own particular stages—if only the touring stage manager will explain the problem.

16 Staging a one night stand

Until quite recently it would not have been necessary to devote a chapter to the single performance, known as the *one night stand*: a passing mention at the end of the touring chapter would have been sufficient. However, there has been a rapid growth in the number of Sunday night performances slotted into a theatre's weekly programme. These performances are given during the changeover weekends of touring theatres and during the non-production weekends in drama repertory theatres. Midweek one night stands are given in multi-use civic halls, and touring theatres occasionally offer a week's season of different single night performances.

One night stands do not normally carry scenery and any rehearsing is limited to a short band call and sound balance. A major problem for the host stage is lack of advance notification of requirements. This is aggravated by the tendency of performers to arrive so close to curtain time that there is a last-minute scramble to complete preparations for the performance and the standard suffers as a result.

The casual attitude towards preparing to meet the audience is most obvious with pop groups, although it is sometimes to be found in other stars who have acquired their popular reputation in media outside the live theatre. Pop groups tour extensive sound equipment and the loudspeaker stacks form the scenic surround. The better organised tours carry their own lighting equipment, often suspended from 'genie towers' which are raised from stage level by compressed air bottle. The problem for the resident stage staff is knowing whether a group is going to turn up with equipment or not. Groups have *road managers* (in jargon, *roadies*) but the word 'manager' in this context can be misleading because a roadie's function is far more concerned with humping equipment than with management. Any specialist knowledge is usually confined to sound equipment.

But the majority of one night stands consist of *An Evening with Miss X* or *Mr Y in Concert*. The star's solo act forms the second part of the evening and before the interval there are supporting acts. If there is an orchestra, it is usually on stage. To cope with all these shows (and the seemingly endless *country and western* bills that fill the house in some parts of the country) a theatre needs to have a stock staging answer available. If there is an advance call for specific requirements—fine; but if there is no call, then a framework is available to accept most types of performance and give some sort of air of professional presentation.

Stage setting

The basis of the one night stand stage setting is masking drapes in the form of legs, borders, and a backdrop. The side masking should be legs running on and off stage rather than up and down stage, to simplify performers' entrances and to permit side lighting. If this masking box is made fairly big (i.e. legs in line with the proscenium opening or false proscenium if there is one) it can be narrowed down by flats. In many cases black is the most useful colour for the masking but it can be gloomy for certain types of entertainment. A good solution is to have a series of coloured velour-covered flats which can set on french braces to shape the acting area and colour it. An optional sky cloth hanging upstage of the back masking is useful for playing colour and the best type is the backlit plastic cloth known as an *Isora*. A *slash* of silver foil strips is useful as an alternative backing. A set of running tabs on a downstage tabtrack (in the normal variety 'No 1 runners' position) is essential and these tabs should be rich but pale-toned to enable them to accept wide variations in coloured light. Assorted rostra should be available for drum kits, etc. and a couple of small trucked rostra are useful for getting things like guitar amplifiers on and off in a hurry. A set of elegant music stands (with lights) improves the look of an onstage orchestra.

Lighting

The lighting requirement is a series of colour washes with some pale lavender or white for comedy and other full-ups. The battens, footlights and floods of old style stage lighting did this automatically without any adjustments being required to the equipment. Spotlight rigs do the job much more neatly but require adjustment. A one night stand rarely has the time or money available for a conventional lighting rehearsal. The quick, effective way to get colour washes is to drop the lighting bars to stage level, colour them exotically and set every lamp to light vertically downwards (this is the one focusing operation that can be done with any certainty when the bar is away from its ultimate dead). When flown out they will give interesting downlight washes without further adjustment—and the light is only on the performers, not splashed all over the set.

Cross light from stands or towers can add further interest and flexibility in picture composition. The FOH lighting can include pale tints for full-ups plus some saturated colour for the running tabs. The FOH can even be set while they are being coloured, and if necessary when they are all alight: finicky setting of areas is not required, basically it is just a case of soft edge focus and dropping of the sky cloth. Limes pick out the stars and the stage lighting gives a general but controllable colour ambience. An Isora plastic skycloth is lit from behind by a set of strong colours in a batten or flood bar at the top and a different selection of colours in a groundrow at the bottom. Patterns can be made with spotlights on stands behind the Isora; the translucence of the plastic generally softens everything so again there is a possibility of setting roughly to save time. A great virtue of an Isora is that, since all the light is behind, any object or person in front shows up as a clean silhouette.

Some performers supply variety-style plots, others just say 'leave it to you'. It can be fun. Especially when a music number has a slow introduction, the operator fades down to a moody light expecting a sad ballad; then suddenly the music goes up tempo without warning. Getting into a bright light smoothly as if it had been plotted that way is a test of anyone's skill in both board operating and instant lighting design.

Bus and truck

In North America there is a highly developed system of touring shows for stops of one, two or three nights. The show is completely self-contained and even a full musical can fit up in a couple of hours. Europe could learn a lot from these techniques.

17 Staging the amateur production

There are no really fundamental differences between staging amateur and professional productions. The problem for both is basically one of *time*. At the final run-through in the rehearsal room, both are (or should be) in exactly the same state of readiness. However, when it comes to integrating the show with the technical apparatus of the stage, the amateur is at a further disadvantage in that, apart from the weekend, all the technical and dress rehearsing must be accomplished in the evenings only. This must be taken into account during planning and must obviously affect the degree of complexity in the staging that can be aimed for.

The average stage facilities available to the amateur company are likely to be less than those taken for granted by the professional: nevertheless, it should be borne in mind that professional companies frequently work (sometimes through necessity, often through choice) with very simple staging. This does not remove the need for organisation: even if the staging consists only of a plank and a passion, the plank has to be designed, constructed, transported, set-up, lit, and integrated with the passion of the actors.

Therefore, although much of this book is written in terms of the professionally staffed theatre, the areas for decision and the procedures for organisation apply to *all* theatres: specific application to the problems of staging the amateur show is mainly a matter of scale.

Budgeting

The important point in budgeting is not the obvious one that the actors and staff do not get paid, but that the box office income is restricted by the shortness of the run. The money available for staging will therefore be very limited after essentials like author's royalties and hire of the hall have been met. But no matter how small the available sum, there should be an agreed proportional allocation between various departments.

Scheduling

There is no difference in the importance of scheduling or in the basic principles to be observed in allocating the available time.

Scenery

Unless an amateur company is performing in a professional theatre—a situation more common with operatic societies than dramatic ones—the average stage facilities will be much less than the professional takes for granted. A fly tower is just a dream and even a decent suspension system is a luxury. Wing space tends to be minimal and rented stages often have severe restrictions on making temporary modifications to the standard equipment installation. And that equipment installation may be more than merely inadequate—it may well be a positive hindrance. Scenery can rarely come down from the flys and any-

A small amateur theatre, The Talisman, Kenilworth.

thing going off to the sides probably has to break down into single flats because of the lack of wing space. The most successful answer to the small stage (although not always the most frequently used) is the permanent non-realistic framework with furniture and an occasional representational shape to evoke the location. The answer to the multi-set play is certainly not full-size flats getting entangled with borders and lights in a quick scene change. And if the stage is particularly small and nasty, might it not be better to put some of the audience there and play in the round on the hall floor?

Props

Organisation is standard but shortness of run indicates borrowing as the normal means of acquisition.

Lighting

The paper planning is still the same whether the show be amateur or professional. There will be less equipment but that is all the more reason for careful planning of the precise use of each

Many of the most imaginative experimental theatre buildings are now to be found in schools, such as this at Rowlinson School, Sheffield.

instrument: there is no alternative to preparing a lighting rigging plan and a cue synopsis.

Sound

Playing effects through a domestic tape recorder is trickier than with special decks but if the leaders are clearly marked it can be done—and there are a lot of sound enthusiasts about these days who are willing to have a go at doing it. Reinforcement should only be required for big halls with musicals (not for Gilbert and Sullivan, please). Treat hall sound installations with respect, because they may be basically public address systems with a quality more suitable for speech than singing.

Wardrobe

Same organisation required.

Stage management and staff

Amateur companies are usually like the smaller professional companies where the stage management not only organise but 'do'. There is not usually the same breakdown into specialist departments: everyone mucks in. In some amateur societies the backstage workers, particularly lighting, take their own cues from watching the script and the action rather than from a co-ordinating stage manager. This often introduces problems with cues being mistimed or just plain missed. There is a lot to be said for having a stage manager who gives all the cues.

Technical and dress rehearsals

The success of dress rehearsals in an amateur company depends enormously on the director and stage manager keeing cool and spreading an air of confidence. There is every chance that the company will include one or two inexperienced people unused to the chaos of dress rehearsals. We all know that order will ultimately prevail—but *their* confidence needs a boost to see them through. An amateur company is unlikely to be playing in repertoire, but otherwise the procedures are the same with the main problem being not having the day time to sort out problems between consecutive evening dress rehearsals.

Amateur show in a professional theatre

In general, professional theatres enjoy their annual visit from the town's operatic society. It is not just the break from routine. It is often the only week in the year when there is a big company on the stage and a big orchestra in the pit: it is often a theatre's only link with its former glories. For smooth rehearsals and per-formances it is essential that the society's stage manager familiarise himself in advance with that particular theatre's method of cueing. For a clean get-in and fit-up, the key is full advance discussion with the resident stage manager and chief electrician: they are generally very willing to help—remember, most of the theatre staff will have friends and relations in the chorus.

Glossary

Acting area The area of the stage setting within which the actor performs. Also an obsolete type of fixed focus lighting instrument used for downlighting.

Apron A part of the stage projecting towards or into the auditorium. In proscenium stages, the part of the stage in front of the main house curtain.

ASM Assistant stage manager.

Band call Any orchestral rehearsal but particularly a musical (i.e. non-acting) rehearsal of performers with orchestra.

Barndoor Four shutter rotatable device which slides into the front colour runners of fresnel spotlights to shape the beam and reduce stray scatter light.

Battens Lengths of timber at the tops and bottoms of cloths. Also timbers used to join flats together for flying as a french flat (q.v.). Also lengths of overhead flood lighting equipment arranged in 3 or 4 alternating circuits for colour mixing.

Beamlight Lighting instrument with no lens but with parabolic reflector giving a parallel beam.

Bifocal spot Profile spot with additional set of shutters to allow combinations of hard and soft edges from the same lantern.

Black light UV (q.v.).

Board Contraction of switchboard or dimmerboard. The central control point for the stage lighting.

Boom Vertical pole, usually of scaffolding diameter, for mounting lighting instruments.

Boom arm Bracket for fixing lighting instruments to a boom.

Borders Neutral or designed strips of material hung horizontally above the stage to form a limit to the scene and mask the technical regions above the performance area.

Border lights American term for battens.

Box set Naturalistic setting of complete room built from flats with only the side nearest the audience (the 'fourth wall') missing. Often complete with ceiling.

Brace Angled support for scenery. The standard adjustable-length brace hooks into a screw-eye on the flat and is either weighted to the floor or attached by a special large stage screw. See also *French brace*.

Brail To pull a flying piece upstage or downstage from its natural free-hanging position by means of short rope lines attached to the ends of the fly bar.

Breast To pull a flying piece upstage or downstage from its free-hanging position by means of a rope line passed between fly floors and crossing the fly-bar's suspension lines.

Bridge An access catwalk passing across the stage or the auditorium ceiling—usually for lighting. Also used to describe stage floor sections which can be raised or lowered.

Build To construct a scene from its constituent parts. Also an increase in light intensity.

Bump out Australian term for get-out (q.v.).

Bus and truck American term for a tour specially designed for short stops (often 1, 2 or 3 nights).

Call A notification of a working session (e.g. rehearsal call). A request for an actor to come to the stage as his entrance is imminent, formerly by callboy, now by loudspeaker system in the dressing rooms. An acknowledgment of applause (e.g. curtain call).

Cans Headset of earphones with or without boom microphone, used for communications.

Cardioid A type of directional microphone.

Carousel Kodak 35 mm slide projector with horizontally rotating circular slide magazine.

Casuals Part time temporary staff.

CCTV Closed circuit television used to transmit picture of conductor in pit to off-stage chorus. Also used to transmit picture of stage to audience latecomers waiting in the foyer.

Centre line An imaginary line running from the front to the back of the stage through the exact centre of the proscenium opening.

Chains Hanging chains are used to suspend battened cloths and borders, also lighting bars, from the hanging bars of a counterweight flying system. Slender chain is sometimes used to weight the bottom of gauzes although electric conduit tubing is often preferred as it keeps the gauze stretched.

Channel A sound or lighting control circuit.

Check Decrease in light intensity.

Circuit A complete path from the electrical supply to the lamp. When such a path includes a dimmer, it should be called a channel, but the word 'circuit' is often used loosely to include channel. Also *touring circuit*, a series of theatres visited by touring companies.

Cleat Special piece of timber or metal for tying off rope line—usually in the flys or

on the back of a scenic flat.

Cloth A large area of scenic canvas hanging vertically. Top and sides are normally masked. A *backcloth* completes the rear of a scene. A *frontcloth* hangs well downstage usually to hide a scene change taking place behind.

Colour call A listing of the colour filters required in each lighting instrument.

Counterweights Weights which are placed in the cradle of a flying system to counterbalance the weight of the scenery to be flown.

Cover A term used particularly in opera for a standby or understudy actor.

Crossfade Lighting or sound change where some of the channels increase while other channels decrease.

CSI (Compact Source Iodine) A type of high intensity discharge lamp (cannot be dimmed electrically).

Cue The signal that initiates a change of any kind during a performance.

Cyclorama Plain cloth extending around and above the stage to give a feeling of infinite space. Term is often used for a blue skycloth, either straight or with a limited curve at the ends.

Dark A theatre which is temporarily or permanently closed to the public.

Dayman Permanent full time 'rank and file' member of the staff, e.g. stage dayman, electrics dayman, etc.

Dead The plotted height of a piece of suspended scenery or masking (*trim* in America). Also discarded items of scenery.

Dead lines Suspension lines which are fixed and not able to be raised or lowered via the normal pulley system from the flys.

Designer Responsible for conception and supervision of the execution of the visual aspects of the production. Separate designers may be employed for scenery, costumes, and lighting.

Dimmer Electrical device which controls the amount of electricity passed to a lamp and therefore the intensity of that lamp's brightness.

Dips Small traps in the stage floor giving access to electrical sockets (known as *floor pockets* in America).

Director Has the ultimate responsibility for the interpretation of the script through his control of the actors and supporting production team.

Discharge lamps Special high-powered light sources whose use is restricted to follow spots and projection because of difficulties in remote dimming by electrical means.

Dock (see scene dock).

Double handling Moving scenery or equipment more than necessary because it was not properly positioned in the first instance.

Double purchase Counterweight flying system where the cradle travels half the distance of the fly bar's travel and therefore leaves the side wall of the stage under the fly galleries clear of flying equipment.

Downstage The part of the stage nearest to the audience.

Dresser Helps actors with costume care and costume changing during the performance.

Dress parade Prior to the first stage dress rehearsal, the actors put on each of their costumes in sequence so that the director and designer can check the state of preparedness of the wardrobe department.

Drift The length of suspension wire between the counterweight bar and the top of the piece to be flown.

Electrics The members of the electrical department. Also all electrical equipment.

Elevator stage Type of mechanical stage with sections which can be raised or lowered.

Ellipsoidal Strictly, a type of reflector used in many profile spotlights but extended in America as a word to cover all profile spots.

Enclosure The housing or cabinet which contains loudspeaker units.

Equalisation Series of controls on a sound mixer for adjusting the tonal quality.

Equalisation cut A switch on the sound mixer to allow the equalised tonal quality to be compared with the original non-equalised sound.

False proscenium A portal (q.v.) particularly one in the downstage areas.

False stage A special stage floor laid for a production to allow trucks, guided by tracks cut into the floor, to be moved by steel wires running in the shallow (two or three inches) void between the false and original stage floors.

Feedback (see Howlround).

Fit up The initial assembly on the stage of a production's hardware, including the hanging of scenery, building of trucks, etc. Also the installation of production lighting (*electrics fit-up*).

Flash out Checking whether lighting instruments are working by switching them on one at a time.

Flats Lightweight timber frames covered with scenic canvas. Now often covered with plywood and consequently no longer light weight.

Floats Jargon for footlights.

Flood Simple lighting instrument giving a fixed spread of light.

Flys The area above the stage into which scenery can be hoisted out of sight of the audience.

Fly floors High working platforms at the sides of the stage from which the flying lines are handled.

Flyman Technician who operates the scenery suspension system above the stage.

Fly tower High structure above the stage which contains the flys (q.v.).

Focus Strictly speaking, the adjustment to give a clearly defined image; but often used to cover the whole process of adjusting the direction and beam of spotlights (in which the desired image may be anything but clearly defined).

FOH Front-of-house—everything on the audience side of the proscenium, particularly the lighting.

Foldback Sound reinforcement from loudspeakers on the side of the stage to enable actors to hear their musical accompaniments clearly, and to hear their own voices when the sound is heavily reinforced for the audience.

Follow spots Spotlights with an operator used to follow actors around the stage.

Footlights Long strip of flooding equipment along the front edge of the stage, arranged in three or four circuits for colour mixing.

Forestage The area in front of the house

curtain on a proscenium stage.

French brace Timber non-adjustable brace (q.v.) usually attached to a scenic flat by a pin-hinge. Often swung flush to the flat on this hinge for packing or flying.

French flat A scenic flat which is flown into position.

Fresnel spot Spotlight with soft edges due to fresnel lens which has a stepped moulding on the front and a textured surface on the back.

Front cloth A cloth (q.v.) hanging at the front of the stage. Also a variety act which can perform in the shallow depth of stage in front of a frontcloth.

Frost A diffuser filter used to soften the beam from a lighting instrument.

FUF Full-up-finish. An increase to bright light over the last couple of bars of a musical number.

Fuse Protective device for an electrical circuit, either cartridge or piece of special wire which melts when the rated electrical current is exceeded.

Gauze Fabric with holes which becomes transparent or solid under appropriate lighting conditions (*Scrim* in America).

Gels Jargon for colour filters although they are no longer manufactured from gelatine.

Get-in Unloading a production into the theatre.

Get-out Dismantling a production and loading it on to transport for removal from the theatre.

Gobo A mask placed in the gate of a profile spotlight to shape the beam. It is a simple form of outline projection.

Green The part of the stage area visible to the audience.

Green room Room adjacent to the stage (i.e. the green) for the actors to meet and relax.

Grid The arrangement of wooden or metal slats above which are mounted the pulley blocks of the flying system.

Gridded Any flying piece raised as high as possible into the flys, i.e. to the limit of travel of the set of flying lines.

Groundrow (Electrics) Three- or four-coloured flooding equipment similar to the footlights or batten and placed on the stage floor, usually masked by a scenic groundrow.

Groundrow (Scenic) A piece of scenery standing on the stage floor, often only a couple of feet or so high.

Gun microphones Very directional microphones for use at longer range—effective at up to about three times the distance of a normal cardioid microphone (q.v.).

Hallkeeper Stage door keeper.

Hemp Rope used for flying. The term is used generally to cover all flying systems without counterweights.

Hemp house A theatre where the flying is brute-force manual, without mechanical advantage from counterweights.

HMI A type of high intensity discharge lamp used in scenic projection and follow spots (cannot be dimmed electrically).

HOD Head of department, particularly a theatre's resident stage manager, master carpenter and chief electrician.

Hook clamp A clamp for fixing a lighting instrument to a horizontal bar.

Housekeeper Supervisor of a theatre's cleaning staff.

Houselights The decorative lighting in the auditorium.

Howlround High pitched squeal (sometimes called feedback) when a microphone picks up acoustically from a loudspeaker to which it is connected electrically.

Hyper-cardioid A very directional type of microphone.

Instrument A lighting unit used for stage lighting such as spotlight or flood. An American term but coming into general use. See *also Lantern, Lamp and Luminaire.*

Iris An adjustable circular diaphragm to alter the gate size in a profile spot. Also the muscular-operated diaphragm in the human eye which adjusts the eye's aperture to changing light intensities.

Isora A plastic sky cloth, lit from behind.

Jack field Patching system used mainly in sound where the inputs and outputs are female sockets linked by short cords with male plugs.

Ladder Framework in the shape of a ladder (but not climbable) for hanging side lighting.

Lamp The light source within a lighting instrument but sometimes used as an alternative to the words instrument, lantern, spotlight, etc.

Lantern A lighting instrument.

Legs Vertical strips of fabric used mainly for masking, either permanent or neutral.

Leko American for a particular manufacturer's brand of ellipsoidal profile spotlight. Use often extended to all makes of ellipsoidal.

Lifts (see *elevator stage*).

Limes Jargon for follow spots and their operators.

Line source A column of loudspeakers mounted vertically in a long slender enclosure (cabinet).

Linnebach A form of shadow scenic projector.

Load out American term for get-out (q.v.).

Luminaire The international word for any lighting instrument of any kind (not just special lighting instruments as used in theatre).

Marking Placing small discreet marks on the stage floor (temporarily with tape, more permanently with paint) to aid the positioning of scenery and props during a change.

Marking out Sticking tapes to the rehearsal room floor to indicate the geographical plan of the scenery.

Masking Neutral material or scenery which defines the performance area and conceals the technical areas.

Master carpenter Senior member of the scenery staff in the theatre. Also senior carpenter in the workshops.

Mechanist Alternative term (particularly Australia) for stage carpenter and stage hand—i.e. technicians responsible for handling scenery on the stage.

Memory Advanced lighting control systems where the intensities of each lamp for each cue are filed automatically in an electronic store.

Mixer Desk for controlling the quantity, quality, and balance of electronically processed sound.

MD Musical director or conductor.

OP Opposite prompt side of the stage —i.e. stage right (actor's right when facing the audience).

Pan Movement from side to side of a lighting instrument (as opposed to the up and down movement called *tilt*). Also the directional movement of sound by cross-fading from one loudspeaker to another.

Pan cues Electronically reproduced sound effects. A term still occasionally but decreasingly used. Dates from the time when effects were played on a twin turntable disc machine called a panatrope.

Patching A sort of central 'telephone exchange' where lighting dimmers can be connected to appropriate socket outlets around the stage. The term has a similar use in sound for connecting alternative microphone inputs and loudspeaker outputs.

Perches Lighting positions immediately behind the proscenium at each side of the stage. In older theatres there are a series of platforms in these positions.

Perruquier Specialist in making and/or dressing wigs.

PFL A control on a sound mixer channel which allows the operator to listen in advance to the channel to check that it is working or that the actor is standing by.

Piano dress Rehearsal in costume and with all technical facilities but using piano as a substitute for orchestra so that the director can concentrate on movement and technical problems rather than musical ones.

Pilots Low intensity or blue lights around the sides of the stage which do not illuminate the acting area but allow actors and technicians to move about safely. See *also working lights*.

Pin hinge Hinge with removeable pin used to join two pieces of scenery together (one half of the hinge is on each piece of scenery).

Pipe American term for bar, particularly bar on which lighting equipment is hung.

Plot A listing of preparations and actions required during a performance. Each staging department prepares such plots as are required by the individual department's members.

Practical Anything (particularly props and electrics) which has to work realistically rather than merely look realistic.

Preset Anything which is positioned in advance of its being required—such as props placed on the set before the performance, or a scene set behind a back-cloth, or lighting or sound control desk with facilities to set levels in advance of a cue.

Production manager Responsible for the technical preparation, including budgeting, of new productions.

Profile spot A spotlight which projects a profile or outline of any chosen shape and with any desired degree of hardness/softness of the edges (in America often called *leko* or *ellipsoidal*).

Progress shots Sequence of photographs of stage settings and actors used to assist accurate revival of productions.

PS Prompt side of the stage—stage left (actor's left when facing the audience).

Prompt book Master copy of the script, containing all actor moves and technical cues, used by the stage management to control the performance.

Props (properties) Furnishings, set-dressings, and all items large and small which cannot be classified as scenery, electrics or wardrobe.

Proscenium theatre The traditional form of theatre where the audience sit in a single block facing the stage and there is a fairly definite division between audience and stage. The position of this division is known as the *proscenium* and takes many forms from a definite arch, not unlike a picture frame, to an unstressed termination of the auditorium walls and ceiling.

Pyrotechnics Bombs, bangs, flashes, etc., usually fired electrically.

Reinforcement Increasing the level of sound by electronic amplification.

Repertoire A form of organisation where two or more productions alternate in the course of a week's performances.

Repertory A form of organisation, usually with a permanent company of actors, where each production has a run of limited length. At any time there is normally one production in performance, another in rehearsal, and several in varying degrees of planning.

Repetiteur Pianist and vocal coach in an opera house.

Resident stage manager Title given, mainly in touring theatres, to the master car-penter. Responsible to the theatre manager for the staff and the building, and to the touring manager for provision of performance facilities.

Rifle microphones See gun microphones.

Ring intercom Communication system linking all technical areas by means of plugging boxes for headsets.

Riser The vertical part of a step. Also a microphone which can be raised through a small trap in the stage floor to a convenient height for the actor.

Road manager (roadie) A touring technician with one-night-stands, particularly pop groups.

Rostrum A portable platform usually in the form of a collapsible hinged framework with a separate top.

Run A sequence of performances of the same production (e.g. long run).

Runners A pair of curtains parting at the centre and moving horizontally, particularly these used in the downstage position in variety and revue productions.

Saturation rig A type of lighting installation in a repertoire theatre where the maximum number of spotlights is positioned in every available position.

Scatter Low-intensity light cast outside the main beam of a spotlight.

Scene dock High-ceilinged storage area adjacent to the stage.

Scrim American term for gauze (q.v.).

Segue Musical term for an immediate follow on. Often used as jargon for any kind of immediate follow on.

Setting line A line, usually just upstage of the house curtain and parallel to the front of the stage, from which all positions for the scenery are measured.

Showman Part-time member of staff engaged for performances only.

Sightlines Lines drawn on plan and section to indicate limits of audience vision from extreme seats, including side seats and front and back rows.

Single purchase Counterweight flying system where the cradle travels the same distance as the fly bar's travel. The counterweight frame therefore occupies the full height of the side wall of the stage.

Sitzprobe Opera house term for a rehearsal

with orchestra where the cast sing but do not act.

Slash Shiny foil strips hanging from a bar and giving the appearance of a metallic cloth slashed into a series of vertical strips about 2 in wide.

Spill Stray or scatter light outside the main beam of a spotlight.

Spotlight A lighting instrument giving control of the angle of the emerging light beam and therefore of the size of area lit.

Spot line A temporary line dropped from the grid to suspend something in an exact special position.

Sprinklers Devices which release water automatically in the event of fire.

Staff director Member of the production staff in a repertoire theatre responsible for maintaining the standard of a production in the repertoire, including revivals and cast changes. Usually was the assistant director on the original rehearsals of the production.

Stage director Formerly the senior member of the stage management team but title now rarely used in order to avoid confusion with the *director*.

Stage manager In overall control of the performance with responsibility for signalling the cues that co-ordinate the work of the actors and technicians.

Stagione A form of repertoire with a very small range of productions in performance at any given time where each production is given intense rehearsal followed by a burst of performances close together, then placed in store. Each revival is rehearsed almost as if it were a new production.

Standing Scenery ('standing set') or lights ('standing light') which does not change during the performance.

Strobe Device giving a fast series of very short light flashes under which action appears frozen.

Tabs Originally 'tableaux curtains' which drew outwards and upwards, but now generally applied to any curtain including a vertically flying front curtain (house tabs), and especially a pair of horizontally moving curtains which overlap at centre and move outwards from the centre.

Tab track Track with centre overlap for suspending and operating horizontally moving curtains.

Talkback Two-way communication, usually of the type where one station (e.g. prompt corner) is a master station which can always speak but can choose by a switch whether to listen to any reply.

Tallescope Alloy vertical ladder on an adjustable wheeled base.

Technical director (administrator/ manager) Co-ordinates and budgets the work of all technical departments.

Theatre-in-the-round A form of staging where the audience totally encircle the acting area.

Throw The distance between a light and the actor or object being lit.

Thrust Form of stage which projects into the auditorium so that the audience are seated on at least two sides.

Thyristor Modern electronic device which has become the standard dimmer.

Tilt Vertical (up/down) movement of a lighting instrument. (See also *pan*.)

Topping and tailing Cutting out the dialogue and action between cues in a technical rehearsal.

Tormentors Narrow masking flats at right angles to the proscenium.

Transformation A magical scene change where one scene melts into another, often by the use of lights on gauzes/scrims.

Trim The height above stage level of a hanging piece of scenery or masking. Mainly American (the equivalent in Britain is one of the meanings of *dead*).

Tripe. Several cables from a lighting bar taped together from the end of the bar until the point where they are plugged into the socket outlets of the permanent wiring installation.

Truck Castored platform on which a scene or part of a scene is built to speed up scene changing.

Tumbling Flying a cloth from the bottom as well as from the top when there is insufficient height to fly in the normal way.

Tungsten lamps Normal lamps whose tungsten filaments gradually lose the brightness of their light output. The stage types are the big brothers of standard domestic lamps.

Tungsten halogen lamps Special lamps

which maintain their initial brightness of light output throughout life.

Upstage The part of the stage furthest from the audience.

UV Ultra violet light (from which harmful radiations have been filtered out) used to light specially treated materials which fluoresce in an otherwise blackened stage.

Wagon stage Mechanised stage where the scenery is moved into position on large sliding platforms as wide as the proscenium opening and stored in large areas to the sides and rear of the main stage.

Wardrobe General name for the costume department, its staff, and the accommodation that they occupy.

Wardrobe maintenance The division of the wardrobe department responsible for the day-to-day cleaning, pressing and running repairs.

Wardrobe plot Actor-by-actor, scene-by-scene, inventory of all the costumes in a production giving a detailed breakdown into every separate item in each costume.

Ways The number of channels in a lighting control system.

Wings The technical areas to the sides of the acting area. Also, scenery standing where the acting area joins these technical areas.

Wipe Single curtain moving across the stage on a single track (*wipe track*) rather than a pair of curtains on a tabtrack (q.v.).

Working lights Stage lights independent of the main dimming system. Switched from the prompt corner but sometimes with overriding switch in the control room in case the prompt corner forgets to switch them off after a scene change.

Further reading

Costume
James Laver: *Concise History of Costume* (Thames and Hudson, London)
James Laver: *Costume in Theatre* (Harrap, London)*
'Motley': *Designing and Making Stage Costumes* (Studio Vista, London)*
Nevil Truman: *Historic Costuming* (Pitman, London)*

Lighting
Frederick Bentham: *The Art of Stage Lighting* (A & C Black, London: Theatre Arts Books, New York)
Richard Pilbrow: *Stage Lighting* (Cassell, London; Drama Book Specialists, New York)
Francis Reid: *The Stage Lighting Handbook* 2nd edition (A & C Black, London; Theatre Arts Books, New York)

Props
Warren Kenton: *Stage Properties and How to Make Them* (A & C Black, London)
'Motley': *Theatre Props* (Studio Vista, London;* Drama Book Specialists, New York)

Scenery
Michael Warre: *Designing and Painting Stage Scenery* (Studio Vista, London)*
Chris Hoggett: *Stage Crafts* (A & C Black, London)
Howard Bay: *Stage Design* (Pitman, London;* Drama Book Specialists, New York)

Sound
David Collison: *Stage Sound* (Cassell, London; Drama Book Specialists, New York)

Stage Management
Hendrik Baker: *Stage Management and Theatrecraft* (J G Miller)
Bert Gruver (revised Hamilton): *The Stage Manager's Handbook* (Drama Book Specialists, New York)

* Titles with an asterisk are unfortunately no longer in print (although please note that in some cases a US edition is still available), but you may be able to find them in libraries.

Index